WHO GETS THE SILVER?

WHO GETS THE SILVER?

AN OLD-SCHOOL INTERACTIVE GUIDE TO ESTATE PLANNING DECISIONS

JULIE KESTER

KESTER PUBLISHING
LAS CRUCES, NEW MEXICO, USA

Published by Kester Publishing
Las Cruces, New Mexico, USA

ISBN 978-1-468-11753-0

Typesetting services by BOOKOW.COM

CONTENTS

Introduction   1

Part One: Getting Started   3

Your Role in the Estate Planning Process 3

Why is it So Hard to Get Motivated? 5

A Very Brief Primer on Estate Planning and Administration 10

    Typical Estate Planning Documents 10

    The Truth About Probate 11

    A Plan in Action 12

Part Two: Roles   16

Executor 16

    What The Role Entails 17

    Time Involved 17

    Your Starter List 18

    Narrow Down Your List - Factors to Consider 19

    A What? What's a Professional Fiduciary? 21

    How to Choose a Professional Fiduciary 22

    Consider Co-Executors 24

    Your Final List 24

Guardian 25

    What The Role Entails 25

    Your Starter List 26

    Naming a Couple 27

    Narrow Down Your List - Factors to Consider 28

    Your Final List 32

    Specifying People Who Shouldn't Act 32

    Couples Who Can't Agree 33

Trustee 33

    What the Role Entails 33

    Your Starter List 35

    Narrow Down Your List - Factors to Consider 35

    Remember the Professional Fiduciary Option 38

    What About Co-Trustees? 38

Your Final List 39
Attorneys-in-Fact (Agents) 39
    Property Agent 39
    Health Care Agent 41

Part Three: Distribution Plan   **44**
What Do I Own? 44
    Figuring Out Your Net Worth 45
    Untitled Assets 47
    Loans to children 48
    Orphan assets 48
    Collections 50
Who Gets My Stuff? 52
    Personal Property 52
    Specific Monetary Bequests 60
    Residue 61
When and How Do They Get It? 77
    Types of Control 77
    Provisions for Spouses 82
    Provisions for Children 85
    Provisions for Charities 90
    Trusts for Education 91
Summarizing Your Plan 93

Part Four: Making the Plan a Reality   **94**
Do You Need a Lawyer? 94
    Factors to Consider 95
    Choosing a Lawyer 96
    Going It Alone 100
    Working With Your Lawyer (If You Use One) 100
"Bulletproof" Your Plan 101
Executing Your Documents 104
Document Storage and Distribution 105
Review Schedule 106
Communicating Your Plan 107

Conclusion   **109**

Appendices   **110**
Appendix A: Estate Plan Blueprint 111
Appendix B: Communication Checklists 129
Appendix C: Assets and Liabilities 131
Appendix D: Information for Guardian 138
Appendix E: Information for Executor 141
Appendix F: Cheat Sheet 142

INTRODUCTION

Have you picked up a book on estate planning lately? There are many to choose from; they explain how documents work, why you should avoid probate, and how tax planning techniques can potentially save you thousands (if not millions) of dollars. What they *don't* explain—at least beyond a brief mention—is how to make the very basic decisions that need to be made before you can even start talking about strategies. Who should get your assets when you die? What qualities should you look for in a trustee? How do you keep your family from fighting after you're gone?

This guide will help you answer those and many other questions which form the heart of an estate plan. Theoretically, you and your attorney could walk through these topics together as part of the estate planning process; however, two factors usually prevent that from occurring: Your attorney doesn't have the time to spend several hours with you on non-legal advice, and you don't want to pay your attorney for several hours of non-legal advice. This book costs less than you would pay for five minutes of a typical attorney's time and attention (a bargain!) and it allows you to work through issues at your own pace. It also allows you to give the issues the careful thought they deserve without any pressure.

So what's an "old-school interactive guide?" "Old school" means no technological wizardry—we'll be using good old paper and pen(cil)—and "interactive" means you need to get involved. Work through the guide as if we were discussing the issues in person, writing down your responses to questions instead of saying them out loud, and before you know it your plan will take shape. If you have questions about legal concepts or options, make a note of them in the guide and take it with you when you see your attorney.

Before we dig in, let's get some preliminaries out of the way. First, you should know a little bit about me. I am an estate planning attorney who has helped many clients work through the decisions that you face now. Also, for several years I was an estate administrator at a large bank in the Chicago area; this means that I settled the estates of people who named the bank as their executor or trustee, and it also means that I got to see how their estate plans played out in real life. Seeing both sides of the process gave me some valuable insights into what works and what doesn't work when it comes to estate plans, and those insights are what I bring to you now.

What I do *not* bring to you is legal advice. There are plenty of good resources out there which address legal concepts and issues; this guide is about the non-legal questions that no one seems to address until the last minute, if at all. Experience has taught me that these non-legal questions are the ones that people care about the most.

I also don't bring you legal advice because I can't: I don't know the first thing about you, and odds are that you live in a jurisdiction in which I am neither competent nor licensed to provide legal services. This is an important point, so let's make it our first interactive adventure. Grab a pen and answer the following:

Is Julie going to provide legal advice in this book? ____ No ___ No

There; see how easy that was?

I have tried to strike appropriate balances throughout the guide to make it work for everyone, but compromise can be tough. For example, the guide is written on the assumption that you know very little—but not absolutely nothing—about estate planning. If you know more than a little, feel free to skim through the explanatory sections. If you know absolutely nothing and find yourself getting confused, refer to the Cheat Sheet at the very end of the Appendix; it contains definitions of basic terms that you may find helpful. Similarly, when I ask you to make a list (for example, of prospective executors) and I give you five lines to do it, don't be afraid to leave a line blank or add a couple of extra lines. The goal is for you to make decisions you can live with, not for you to follow my instructions to the letter.

Finally, you will find a number of "true stories" sprinkled throughout the guide which illustrate the topic at hand. These stories are all true, but for obvious reasons (and with one obvious exception), the facts have been tweaked slightly when necessary to protect the identity of the people involved. Former clients and associates need not worry.

PART ONE:
GETTING STARTED

Your Role in the Estate Planning Process

Some people seem to think that an individual's role in the estate planning process is to show up at an attorney's office, answer a few questions, sign some documents, and write a check. Nothing could be further from the truth.

Look at this partial list of issues that are involved in estate planning:

- Choose an executor
- Pull the plug?
- Choose a guardian
- Tax planning
- Who gets my money?
- When do kids get their money?
- Probate avoidance
- Include step-children?
- Choose a health care agent
- What happens to my pets?
- Properly drafted documents
- Who gets Grandma's cameo?
- Include charities?

- Choose a trustee
- Leave something to my ex-spouse?
- Choose a property agent
- Who gets the family cabin?
- Pay for grandkids' education?
- Disinherit Bobby?
- Give back to my school?
- What message do I want to send?

Now we'll organize all of those items into legal decisions (your attorney's job) and personal decisions (your job):

Legal Decisions	Personal Decisions
Properly drafted documents	Choose an executor
Tax planning	Pull the plug?
Probate avoidance	Choose a guardian
	Who gets my money?
	When do kids get their money?
	Include step-children?
	Choose a health care agent
	What happens to my pets?
	Who gets Grandma's cameo?
	Include charities?
	Leave something to my ex-spouse?
	Choose a property agent
	Who gets the family cabin?
	Pay for grandkids' education?
	Disinherit Bobby?
	Give back to my school?
	What message do I want to send?

Do you see the lop-sided division of labor? The law doesn't care whom you name to act as your executor; that is not a legal issue. The law doesn't care how much you want to leave to your church. The law doesn't care if you decide that one of your children needs or deserves a larger inheritance than another. These are personal decisions that you as an individual need to make.

If you don't know what you want when you sit down with your attorney, he or she will try to help you reach decisions on the spot. I do this myself all the time, even though obviously I'm a strong advocate of people taking their time and making their own decisions on non-legal issues. Why do I do it, then? Because I know if a client leaves my office with a list of open items, he or she is likely to put that list on a pile of papers at home and promptly forget about it. Since I believe that a so-so plan on paper is better than a good plan in someone's head, I take the lead and we get the job done.

It shouldn't be that way. *You* need to play the lead role in developing your estate plan, turning to professional advisors and/or your own research to fill in the blanks when necessary. This guide will help you work through the many the decisions you need to make, but it won't give you the answers—those have to come from you.

Why is it So Hard to Get Motivated?

The hardest part of estate planning is getting started, and the second hardest part of estate planning is getting done. If you've picked up this guide, you're already ahead of the curve, but let's make sure that your motivation is sufficient to get you through the process. Think of this as an estate planning pep talk.

Psychologically, estate planning is a tough task for several reasons; some are obvious and some are not. See if any of these strike a chord with you:

Death is not a fun topic. For the most part, estate planning centers around events that people would rather ignore—their own death, the death of a loved one, their physical or mental incapacity, and other similarly unhappy prospects. No parent likes to contemplate his young child growing up as an orphan. No elderly person likes the feeling of preparing for his coming disability or death. No one wants to suffer, and no one wants to cease to exist.

I don't need to tell you that death is going to happen to everyone; you know that. I also don't need to tell you that ignoring an unpleasant truth won't make it go away; if you are reading this, you're old enough to know that that doesn't work. Some day you will not exist on this planet. Some day neither will I. It's the human condition.

Most people are able to suspend their discomfort long enough to get through the estate planning process successfully, but some have more difficulty than others. When I work with those people, I find that it helps to keep the prospect of death somewhat on the ridiculous side. We don't talk about them wasting away from cancer; we talk about them falling off a mountain. One spouse accidentally electrocutes the other during a relaxing soak in a hot tub. Both spouses fall into comas after eating tainted sushi; we flip a coin to see who "wins" and gets to be the survivor. Anything to make the topic of death a little less real and a little more fun.

If you find yourself balking at the mere contemplation of your own death, stop for a second and think of the silliest, most outrageous manner of death you can, and write it here:

Believe it or not, I will die from _____.

Whenever you start to have trouble thinking of yourself as dead, take a deep breath, remind yourself of the incredibly awesome way you went out, and move forward.

No deadline. There is a 100% certainty that you will die eventually, but there is an exceedingly close to 100% certainty that you will not die before you finish reading this guide. In fact, at any point in your life, the odds that you will die tomorrow are extremely low—actuarially speaking, the longer you live, the longer you are likely to live; no one's projected life expectancy is ever equal to zero.

What this means is that there is no knowable deadline associated with estate planning, and that makes it extremely easy to put off. You're thirty years old and in good health; what difference does it make if you get your plan in order now or six months from now? You're fifty-five and in relatively good health; what difference does it make if you get your plan in order now or six months from now? You're seventy-two and following your doctor's orders religiously; what difference does it make if you get your plan in order now or six months from now?

The truth is that it doesn't matter—until it does, and at that point it's too late. Obviously it's too late if you're dead or in an irreversible coma, but it's also too late if you have gradually aged and are now past the point of competence. The threshold for competence when it comes to executing valid estate planning documents is fairly low—you only need to understand in a general way what you have and who your beneficiaries are, and you need to have intent to sign the documents—but waiting until your competence is the least bit in question can be an invitation for a Will contest later.

We humans are not used to working without a deadline, and most of us aren't very good at it. Therefore, since nature doesn't provide advance notice of your demise and there is no boss looking over your shoulder, you need to set a deadline yourself. Now is as good a time as any. For a realistic deadline, give yourself about a month to work through all of your decisions and a couple of months to get your plan drafted and signed. Feel free to set a more aggressive deadline if circumstances warrant or if you're a classic overachiever; you can set a longer deadline if you know your progress will be interrupted by a long vacation or unavoidable delay. The important thing is to commit to a date. Ready? Grab your pen and fill in this statement:

I will have my estate plan complete and signed by _____, 20____.

There. If you take this deadline seriously, then you're on your way.

Nobody likes to deal with the law. Okay, I like to deal with the law, but I'm a lawyer. For most people, legal situations are confusing and intimidating; they know that what they are doing is important but they also know that the document in front of them is dry, full of words they don't understand, and frankly inscrutable. Most people solve the issue by relying on their lawyer to tell them that everything is in order, but that's not a comfortable feeling. What if the lawyer messed up? What if there's language in Article VII, Section A(4)(b) that does the opposite of what you would want? How would you even know?

I'll let you in on a secret: Estate planning documents are so long and dense because estate planning lawyers like certainty. Much of the language in a Will or trust sounds convoluted, but those phrases and passages that sound so stilted to you are there because they work—they were tested and endorsed by a court a million years ago, everyone started using them, and now everyone still uses them because, well, everyone uses them. Wills and trusts are not the place for creative writing; they are the place for writing that lawyers, financial providers, and (most importantly) courts understand and interpret the same way.

True story: When I was a young estate planning associate, one of the partners for whom I worked seemed to have an obsession with the origins of what he called "the language." We had standard form books (everyone does) and I would be tasked with using and adjusting the standard forms to accomplish the client's wishes. Sometimes I couldn't find anything in the form book that came close to meeting the client's requirements; in those cases, I would simply write a section myself. I would sit at the partner's desk as he reviewed my work and wait for the inevitable comment: "Where did you get this language?" I would bristle—I was a trained attorney, I knew how to write, I knew how to think, I could draft a passage that accomplished its goal logically and legally—and mutter something about adapting a section of Form Book X or Court Case Y. One day, though, I had had enough. "I made it up," I said. "Is there something wrong with it?" He brusquely opined that yes, there was something wrong with it—it had not been used before. In the end, he insisted that I find "language" in a form book—*any* form book—that did what needed to be done.

I didn't understand (and most certainly did not agree with) the partner at the time, but now I see his point. Legalese is frustrating and often embarrassingly opaque, but it is reliable. When a document indicates that distributions can be made for a beneficiary's "health, education, maintenance, and support," the phrase carries a specific meaning that has been established over the course of numerous court cases and tax rulings. Could it be stated more clearly from a layman's perspective? Probably, but if I used that "clearer" language I couldn't guarantee that the language would hold up against a court or IRS challenge. I for one am not going to take the chance.

The point of all this is that to get through the estate planning process, you have to be willing to let go a little bit. Trust your lawyer. Yes, your lawyer should be able to explain the effect of any passage that you ask about, but you should feel comfortable with a general explanation. If you don't, you may be working with the wrong lawyer.

Estate planning can prompt unpleasant life assessment. Each of us has parts of our life that don't measure up to what we expected; it's inevitable. The estate planning process entails taking stock of all areas of your life, including the less-than-perfect ones. Maybe you don't have as much wealth as you expected you would. Maybe your children aren't turning out the way you had hoped, or maybe you don't have children at all and wish you did. Not many of us are blessed with a huge net worth and a perfect personal life.

Don't be surprised if this process makes you a little bit depressed from time to time, but don't let that stop you. True story: I once had a client who was obviously dragging her feet; she kept telling me we needed to meet and get her plan done, but she kept dodging every opportunity to do so. Finally one day I ran into her at the grocery store (of all places) and asked her point blank what was holding her up. "Simple," she said. "I have nothing and I have no one to give it to anyway." She laughed, but on some level she was serious. This was a person who was having significant trouble looking at her life in the cold light of day.

I tell you this only to alert you to the possibility that you may have some of the same feelings. If you find yourself making increasingly dubious excuses to avoid thinking about the topics raised in this guide, I would respectfully suggest that you need to give yourself a break. You're doing the best you can, just like all of us.

This is hard stuff. Estate planning is all about predicting the future—an ultimately impossible task. Should you leave your children's inheritance to them outright? If so, when? This would be an easy question to answer if you could know what your child is going to be like at age 18, 25, 35, or 45, but you can't. Will he be responsible or immature? Rich or poor? Disabled? In the middle of a messy divorce? Will he even still be alive?

The decisions you will make during the course of our journey often don't have a clear-cut answer. There is no right or wrong—or at least you can't know what's right or wrong based upon the information you have today. Each option will have pros and cons, and sometimes the pros and cons of two very different (and mutually exclusive) options may seem painfully equal. This can cause "analysis paralysis" and is a primary reason for the failure to get a plan done.

Don't let that happen to you. Accept the fact that you are going to have to make decisions based on imperfect and incomplete information, and accept the fact that some of those decisions may backfire in the future if life doesn't turn out as you predicted. All you can do is take your best shot.

In the end, who cares? This is perhaps the biggest demotivator of all. If you die without an estate plan, the world will not stop turning. Your assets will end up somewhere—perhaps not exactly where you would have chosen, but they won't just disappear. Your children will grow up somehow whether you have nominated a guardian for them or not. People die intestate (without a Will) every day, and life goes on.

True story: I once knew a man who volunteered his time to a youth organization with some pretty stringent rules: The kids had to wear uniforms, the uniforms had to be clean and crisp, tardiness was not tolerated, and so forth. One day a participant challenged the volunteer, asking why everyone had to follow so many rules. The volunteer replied, "You don't *have* to; you *get* to. Being a part of this group is a privilege."

That's how you should think of estate planning—you don't *have* to make these decisions; you *get* to. You have the right to make decisions that will affect those whom you love even after you die. Don't give up that right.

A Very Brief Primer on Estate Planning and Administration

In order to give you a framework for the decisions you need to make, let's start with a very brief outline of what an estate plan is and how it works. This outline is *not* comprehensive, it is *not* state-specific, and it is *not* meant to provide legal advice. (Is Julie providing legal advice? No.) It is simply a way to get you familiar with the basic process and terminology involved.

Typical Estate Planning Documents

There are only three or four documents that make up a typical estate plan. They are a **Will** (which only takes effect after you die), two **powers of attorney** (which are in effect during your lifetime but cease to be in effect when you die), and in some cases a **trust** (which can take effect during your lifetime or when you die). You can change any or all of these documents at any time during your lifetime unless you become legally incompetent.

Your **Will** controls the disposition of any property you owned individually at the time of your death. (It does not control the disposition of property you owned jointly with another person, property with a designated beneficiary, or property you had already placed in a trust.) Your Will also indicates your wishes regarding who will settle your estate (your executor, personal representative, or administrator; this guide will use the term executor) and who will raise your children (their guardian). Note that the court does not have to follow your wishes with respect to these appointments, but in most cases it will.

Powers of attorney give the person named in the document (called your attorney-in-fact or agent; this guide will use the term agent) the authority to act on your behalf if you cannot do so because of disability. Property powers of attorney give the agent the authority to act on your behalf with respect to financial matters, and health care powers of attorney (also called health directives) give the agent the authority to make medical and health care decisions on your behalf. If you become disabled and both of these documents are in place, you most likely will not have to resort to a court-appointed guardian and conservator; people with whom you need to deal (financial institution, health care facility, etc.) should accept the signed power of attorney as authorization to work with your agent just as he or she would work with you.

Trusts are extremely flexible tools that can work both during your lifetime and after your death. Basically, a trust is a legal entity that can own property and is governed by whatever terms the trust agreement contains. Trusts can be revocable (you can change the terms) or irrevocable (you can't change the terms), they can be created jointly with others or alone, they can dictate what happens to trust property years into the future—the possibilities are (nearly) endless.

The most common type of trust used in estate planning is the revocable trust (also called living trust), and that is the type of trust we will refer to in this guide. If funded properly, a revocable trust allows you to avoid probate (but see below) and also allows you to exercise control more easily over how your assets are used and when they are distributed.

The Truth About Probate

If you own individual property worth over a minimal amount at the time of your death, your estate will "go through probate." This usually is not the horrific experience that people expect. Often using forms supplied by the local court and often with the assistance of an attorney, your executor presents your Will to the court and the court verifies that the Will is valid. (Technically, this is the "probate" part of the process.) The court issues a document that gives your executor the authority to deal with estate assets, your executor deals with the assets and reports back to the court when the work is done, and the court closes the process. If minor children are involved, the court also officially names a guardian for the children and often requires annual check-ins to ensure that the guardian is doing a good job. And that's it.

This is not to say that probate is not worth avoiding if possible. Some legitimate downsides to probate include:

- Added expense. While most jurisdictions do not require attorney involvement in the probate process, most people do retain an attorney to insure that everything is done properly, and while an attorney's work may be limited in a straightforward estate, there will be fees involved. There also likely will be court filing fees and, in some jurisdictions, additional probate fees based on the value of the estate.

- Delay. Different jurisdictions have different rules, but typically the probate matter will need to remain open for several months to a year or more. While most of the actual work can be accomplished early in the process, many people find it unpleasant to have to wait so long before they can feel that everything is done.

- Publicity. The probate process is public, which means that your Will, asset inventory, and so forth can be obtained by anyone with a legitimate interest (which may as well be everyone). As a practical matter, this is rarely an issue; if, however, you are a private person and/or your estate plan contains provisions that you would rather keep private, you should be aware of the possibility of disclosure.

In short, if the rest of your circumstances make it possible or advantageous to own no property in your individual name when you die, then probate avoidance can be a nice side benefit of your plan. In and of itself, however, probate avoidance does not need to be your primary goal.

A Plan in Action

Here's how the administration of an estate might work in practice:

You're crossing the street and you get hit by the proverbial bus. You're in terrible shape but the doctors think they might be able to save your life through a daring, risky experimental procedure. The problem? They need your consent, but you're in a coma.

Your health care agent has the legal authority to consent to treatment on your behalf. Based on the agent's understanding of your wishes, he decides that you would consent to the procedure. The hospital is legally able to proceed based on your agent's consent; no formal guardian needs to be appointed by the court.

The procedure is a success! Well, sort of. You are left with permanent physical and mental disabilities that require around-the-clock care; even if you could speak intelligibly, you're not in a position to make decisions for yourself.

Your health care agent continues to make decisions about your medical care and living arrangements; your property agent steps in to manage your finances. None of this requires court involvement.

The doctors do their best, but eventually your injuries take their toll. Alas, you die. You leave behind a spouse, three children, and (fortunately) a solid estate plan.

Your Will is probated and your executor is given the authority to settle your estate. The executor sues the bus company and obtains a hefty settlement to compensate for your medical expenses and pain and suffering. The settlement fund and a couple of other assets that you owned individually are collected and turned over to the trustee of your revocable trust, who adds them to assets which you already had put into the trust before your death.

Your spouse and children pick up the pieces and go on with their lives.

Your trustee works out a budget with your spouse which allows the family to live comfortably but not extravagantly, just as you would have wanted. The trust assets are invested appropriately and your spouse receives a monthly distribution to cover living expenses as well as additional distributions when circumstances warrant.

The children grow up and establish lives of their own; your spouse eventually remarries and moves to a retirement village in Florida. After several years of golf and early-bird buffets, your spouse passes away.

The remaining funds are divided into three separate trusts, one for each child, and each child's trust receives an equal share of the trust assets. Each share is worth approximately $300,000.

The children's lives have taken very different paths; the eldest owns a small but thriving restaurant, the middle is a teacher, and the youngest is a talented but struggling musician. The trustee works with each child to understand the child's goals and needs and how that child's trust assets can be used for his or her best interests.

*The **eldest** child wishes to use her trust fund to expand the restaurant. After reviewing the business plan and considering this child's probable future needs, the trustee determines that expansion is in the child's best interests. The assets are distributed outright to the child and the trust is terminated.*

*After consulting with the **middle** child, the trustee determines that this child can support himself and his family at a modest but acceptable level and does not need significant additional income. The trust fund is invested for growth, not income, and is available as a safety net in case of emergencies. It helps the middle child pay his children's college expenses when they arise and eventually is distributed outright to those children when their father dies.*

*For the **youngest** child, the trust you set up all those years ago is a real lifesaver. The music business is cruel; this poor kid has almost hit the big time on several occasions, but the breakout never quite came. Shortly after your spouse's death, the child was talked into self-funding the release of a new CD. He handed over everything he owned to his manager—who promptly skipped town. Fortunately, the trustee refused to advance trust funds for the CD release. Music child was able to rely on the trust for support while he got back on his feet and is now doing fine. If he had received his share outright, it would have been gone along with everything else.*

One estate plan, you and your spouse and your children supported successfully with limited court involvement. Score!

Now that you know what the framework looks like, you can see the blanks that you will need to fill in. They are:

- Roles. Whom will you name to act as executor, guardian (if applicable), health care agent, property agent, and trustee (if applicable)?

- Distribution. Who will receive your assets, and how and when will they receive them?

The next two parts of this guide will walk you through the process of filling your roles and determining your distribution pattern. When you're finished, you will be able to start thinking about how you're going to get real documents with real signatures into your life.

PART TWO:
ROLES

There are several roles that need to be filled before your estate plan can be drafted. This part of the guide will explain the function that each role serves and some factors to consider when you're deciding whom to assign to that role. Finishing this section is like casting a movie; having the right people in the right roles makes all the difference.

When counseling my own clients, I try to get them to list three names for each role in the estate plan—their first choice, an alternate in case the first choice can't act, and a back-up alternate in case neither of the first two can act. This to me strikes the right balance between cavalier and obsessive. You are certainly free to name more than three choices if you like; you can also name only two if you really can't come up with a third, but please consider one choice unacceptable. There simply is too great a risk that any one individual will be unable to act when the time comes.

One more point before we get started: Do your best to choose the right people to fill these roles, but don't let this part of the process paralyze you. Any choice is better than no choice; any estate plan is better than no estate plan. Remember the deadline you set for yourself and stick to it.

Executor

The first role to be filled in your estate plan is that of your executor. Unfortunately, since most people have little or no concept of what an executor does, they are understandably at sea when it comes to selecting someone to fill the role. We are about to remedy that situation.

What The Role Entails

The job of an executor is to administer the probate estate of a decedent (dead person). Depending on the size of the estate and the nature of the assets, administration can be as simple as a couple of documents and a few phone calls or it can be a complicated exercise that takes months (if not years) and involves attorneys, accountants, judges, realtors, court hearings, and no end of headaches. Most administrations, of course, fall somewhere in between. As a general rule, your executor will be responsible for seeing that the following things get done:

- All assets are identified;
- All debts are resolved;
- All taxes are reported and paid;
- All of the right people are notified;
- All required legal processes are followed;
- All issues or contests are resolved; and
- All assets ultimately end up where they should be.

Most individuals who act as an executor seek the assistance of a professional for at least some of their duties; they will hire a lawyer to handle court proceedings, an accountant to prepare tax returns, an estate sale vendor to deal with household goods, and most likely a real estate agent to sell the residence if there is a residence to sell. Professionals can help, but the executor still is responsible for making sure that the entire process is completed correctly.

Time Involved

How much time will the executor have to spend? Again, it depends on the size of the estate and the assets involved. Strictly from a number-of-hours standpoint, the most time-consuming task usually is dealing with personal effects (probably the least valuable asset from a monetary perspective, but that's life). Unless a surviving spouse is going to remain in the residence, someone is going to have to spend many hours going through household contents, locating legal documents to give to professionals, making arrangements to sell what can be sold, distributing personal items to appropriate people, and finding a way to discard the rest. Most people find that it takes at least a couple of weekends of dedicated work to complete this task.

If there is a house to sell, the executor will have to arrange for any necessary repairs to get the house into a marketable condition, choose a real estate agent, and work with the agent as offers come in and then through closing. Figure 5–10 hours minimum for this task.

If legal and tax issues need to be resolved and are contracted out to professionals, the executor will still have to meet with the professionals, supply them with any necessary information, and review their work prior to signing off. Depending on the complexity of the situation, this could be another 5–10 hours. If these tasks are not delegated to professionals, they could easily take 20–40 hours of the executor's time.

If complications arise—a disgruntled relative decides to contest the estate plan, critical documents cannot be located, a toxic oil tank is discovered under the house—all estimates go out the window.

Of course, not all estates go haywire. If you have done all of your homework and leave your affairs in good order, a simple estate can be wound up fairly quickly. True story: I recently talked to a gentleman whose elderly father had just passed away. This gentleman was in from out of town and called me on a Thursday to set up an appointment on Monday to discuss the estate. By the time we met on Monday, he had completed literally every task necessary in connection with his father's death and there was nothing further required. We should all be so lucky.

Your Starter List

Most people follow a fairly standard practice when they name their executor—first is the spouse (if there is one), second is the most capable child (if there is one), and third is a brother or brother-in-law. Maybe that's standard practice because it makes sense, but

I suspect it's standard practice because no one gives a lot of thought to the matter until they're sitting in the lawyer's office and the lawyer is waiting for an answer.

You're going to do better than that. We will use the same starting point—people you know and trust—but then we're going to refine the list down to the best candidates based on something more concrete than your gut feeling. First, make an initial list of your top five prospects:

Prospective Executors:

1) _____

2) _____

3) _____

4) _____

5) _____

Narrow Down Your List - Factors to Consider

Now consider these factors as applied to the names on your list:

- Temperament. You want someone who is not easily frustrated and not overly afraid of red tape. Settling an estate can be tedious even if there are no complications.

- Emotional makeup. Everyone is going to be devastated when you die, of course, but some people will handle it better than others. Try not to place the burden of executorship on someone who is likely to be an emotional wreck, even if they seem to be the best choice based on other factors.

- Family friendly. Obviously, you want someone who will work well with your surviving family members. But "family friendly" also means that the choice will not do anything to damage the family dynamic—which means, to be blunt, that you should think twice about naming one of your children to act as your executor. Yes, some families can pull it off, but they are the exception and not the rule. If any two of your children tend not to get along, if any child is estranged (from you or from siblings), if there is any hint of animosity in your family dynamic... Do everyone a favor and choose a non-family member to act.

- Business savvy. Your executor doesn't have to be an attorney—or know anything about the law, really—but he or she should be comfortable reading and signing legal documents and working with professionals. If the thought of sitting in a conference room makes your prospect queasy, you probably should consider someone else.

- Discretion. Your executor is going to be privy to every aspect of your life, from your income tax returns to the contents of your dresser drawers and everything in between. We all have friends and colleagues who are not particularly good at keeping confidences, although they may be good at everything else. Those people might not be a good choice to serve as your executor.

- Life circumstances. Is the person you have in mind in the middle of a bustling career with a houseful of kids and an elderly parent and more commitments than he or she can keep? If so, don't burden that person with responsibility for settling your estate, even if he or she is otherwise the perfect choice and insists that it would be no burden.

- Geography. While a lot of estate administration tasks can be handled from a distance, all else being equal it probably is more efficient to name someone who lives in your community than someone who lives far away. This is especially true if the executor will have to dispose of your home, since selling the home is likely to involve arranging for repairs and working with a local real estate agent. Again, geography shouldn't be your primary parameter, but it is worth considering.

- Willingness to act. Someone on your list may be hesitant or even unwilling to act, perhaps for reasons that are unknown to you. The only way to know is to ask.

Now we are going to apply those factors to your working list. Fill in the boxes below with a Y for yes and an N for no for each candidate:

	#1	#2	#3	#4	#5
Good temperament?					
Emotionally stable?					
Family friendly?					
Business savvy?					
Discreet?					
Time available?					
Local?					
Willing to act?					

Other than geographical location, each of the above factors is essential to a capable executor, so while it's your decision, I would cross off any name that had more than one "No" associated with it. If that leaves you with no one, try to think of more potential candidates; if you find yourself having to stretch to come up with any more names, then consider whether a professional fiduciary might be the best choice.

A What? What's a Professional Fiduciary?

If you're like most people, there was no professional fiduciary on your list of prospective executors. You may not even know that professional fiduciaries exist. In essence, a professional fiduciary is a bank, trust company, or individual who is in the business of settling estates and managing trusts; it handles all of the tasks outlined above and gets paid a fee for its services.

Professional fiduciaries (especially banks and trust companies) tend to get a bad rap in the estate planning world; the perception I have heard is that they are inordinately expensive, not respectful of beneficiaries, and overly inflexible in their practices. I'm sure that each of these complaints has been valid at one time or another, but my experience both as a professional fiduciary and as one working with professional fiduciaries is that for the most part the complaints are overblown. In fact, professional fiduciaries are particularly good at dealing with:

- Family Issues. Professional fiduciaries have experience with family issues; they know how to get help for a struggling widow or mediate lifelong disputes among children, and they can do it fairly and dispassionately. One of the primary problems with naming a child as executor is that the child's actions (even if completely reasonable) may be questioned or resented by his or her siblings. Even if the siblings don't say or do anything overt, the child executor may worry that his or her actions will be met with hostility, and the added worry can bring stress to an already-stressful endeavor.

True story: Actually, an amalgamation of a number of true stories. When I was a professional administrator, it was not uncommon for my bank to be retained to act as executor halfway through an administration that had started with the decedent's child as executor. The family was at odds, tensions were high, and often at the outset I foresaw nothing but headaches. Usually, though, once the bank took over everyone calmed down and the rest of the administration was a breeze. More often than not, our actions were the same actions that had been proposed by the original executor; his proposals were met with hostility, while ours were not. All these families needed was a disinterested third party to get them through the process.

- Tricky assets. Professional fiduciaries are used to dealing with business interests, commercial properties, odd investments, family partnerships, and other non-run-of-the-mill items. Moreover, a professional fiduciary has the resources to accomplish tasks quickly and easily; paperwork that would take a layman executor hours to complete is simply shunted off to the appropriate department and batched with the day's load of tasks. Appraisals are routine. Tax audits are routine. In essence, everything is routine, and routine is a wonderful thing in the world of estate administration.

- No obvious alternative. Some families just don't have anyone who is equipped to take on the responsibility of settling an estate. If you find yourself having to branch out to a distant cousin or bowling buddy to find someone you trust, you might be better off naming a professional fiduciary.

How to Choose a Professional Fiduciary

If you are considering this route, take the time to interview several options (assuming you have several options available to you; many banks have gotten out of the administrator business in the past few years) before making up your mind. Questions you should ask:

- Fee structure. Figure on anywhere from 2% to 5% of the total value of your estate, but make sure you understand if there is a minimum fee or additional fees for certain types of assets.

- Services provided. A professional fiduciary should do everything needed to get the estate settled. Most will hire an outside attorney (generally yours, if you had one) to do any required legal work; some also will hire an outside accountant to prepare tax returns while others have in-house capability. Remember that every outside professional that the professional fiduciary uses will result in additional fees to your estate.

- Who does the work and where they're located. Back in the day, most banks had trust offices located in the geographical areas they served. If you lived in Anytown, USA, the First Bank of Anytown had a trust office right on Main Street and that's where the work got done. Unfortunately, in many cases those offices have been shut down and the work has been moved to larger centrally-located offices that may be nowhere near your location. (Think 1-800-TRUSTEE.) I understand this trend from a business perspective and I'm sure there are very capable people on staff wherever they are, but part of the professional fiduciary's job is (or should be, or at least used to be) helping the beneficiaries get through a rough time. Going out to the house to meet with a widow who got a confusing notice in the mail. Helping the kids divvy up the Hummel collection without fighting. Checking on the house to make sure the real estate agent is doing his or her job. I fail to see how any of that can be accomplished by a fiduciary who is hundreds or thousands of miles off-site, and for that reason, I have a strong bias toward locally-based operations.

- Investment philosophy. It is likely that when you die, you will own many types of assets—stocks, bonds, maybe real estate, maybe collectibles—and the professional fiduciary will be responsible for managing those assets until your estate is distributed. Depending upon your situation, the asset management rules that they follow and how rigidly they follow them may be extremely important to you and your beneficiaries.

Where I worked, our policy was to sell all stock as soon as possible unless all beneficiaries agreed to take their share in kind (i.e., receive shares of stock instead of cash). We did this because it was our responsibility to preserve and protect the value of the beneficiaries' shares of the estate, and we were not about to make a bet on stocks maintaining or increasing their value over the relatively brief timeframe until we could distribute them. (Bonds were different because they could be held to maturity.) Sometimes this made a beneficiary furious, because "everyone" knew that the stocks were undervalued and would increase in value over the short term. Our position was that if that beneficiary could convince all of the other beneficiaries that the stock should be held, then we would honor their request. Otherwise we simply took the risk off the table by selling.

Particularly in the current economic climate, rigid rules may not provide the best result. Should real estate be sold immediately even if the real estate market is unhealthy at the time? Should an art collection be sold in bulk immediately even if more could be realized by a gradual sale? Should one beneficiary who wants instant cash be able to force all other beneficiaries to take the same? Any professional fiduciary is going to be bound by its duty to all, but you should look for one that isn't afraid to think beyond the strict terms of its policy manual from time to time.

Consider Co-Executors

It is possible to achieve the best of both worlds (at least in theory) by naming co-executors—one a family member and one a professional fiduciary. The professional does the heavy lifting, while the family member keeps an eye on the professional and makes sure that on a personal level, everyone is comfortable with what's happening.

It is possible to name individual co-executors (say, your spouse and a trusted family friend), but there rarely is a good reason to do so. One of the co-executors is going to end up doing all the work—division of labor is difficult in an estate administration—so why not simplify matters and just name that person as sole executor? He or she can always seek help when necessary.

Your Final List

It's time to make your decision. If you are going to name an individual executor, write down your top three choices in order of preference; if you're naming a professional executor, just list it as your first choice:

Executor:

1) _____

2) _____

3) _____

Congratulations! Your first role is filled.

Guardian

For people with small children, the decision of whom to name as guardian often is the hardest of all; I have known people who have put off finalizing their estate plans for years (literally) because they couldn't come to agreement. Delay *is* one approach—if you delay long enough, your children will grow up and naming a guardian will become irrelevant—but I think we both know it's a coward's way out.

What The Role Entails

A guardian is an individual appointed by a court to serve as the legal parent of a minor child if the child's biological or adoptive parents cannot act. (Guardians also can be appointed for disabled adults, but for our purposes we will stick to guardians of minor children.) Note that a guardian only will be appointed if the child has *no* biological or adoptive parent capable of acting as parent; if you and your child's other parent are divorced, for example, you cannot effectively nominate someone else to act as guardian of the child in place of the other parent if he or she is still living and able and willing to act.

Legally speaking, should your child become an orphan, the guardian appointed by the court will step into your shoes in every respect: He or she will assume all of the responsibilities of a parent and will be authorized to make all of the decisions and take all of the actions that being a parent entails. You can leave suggestions as to how to raise your child, which schools the child should attend, etc., but the court will not enforce your wishes if the guardian opts to go another route. You really are placing enormous trust in the person you designate.

That said, before we look at some factors to help guide your decision, let's take some of the pressure off. As you probably know but may forget during this process, children are incredibly resilient creatures—they don't need a perfect environment to turn out okay. (If they did, none of us would ever turn out okay.) There is no such thing as a perfect parent, so stop trying to find one buried in your circle of family and friends. Don't reject someone simply because they are flawed in some way.

Your Starter List

Most people start with at least some idea of whom they might want to name as guardian but don't know how to proceed from there. If you have absolutely no idea, refer to this list of typical guardian choices as a prompt:

- one of your siblings
- one of the child's grandparents
- other relative (e.g., your cousin, aunt or uncle, etc.)
- close family friend
- child's godparent
- child's adult sibling

Take a moment now to write down a starter list of people you want to consider for this role. Err on the side of overinclusion; we'll be weeding people out as we go.

Prospective guardians:

1) _____

2) _____

3) _____

4) _____

5) _____

Naming a Couple

If you have a married couple on your list of potential guardians, I strongly suggest that you think harder about your selection. People often wish to name a married couple as guardian of their children; this makes sense until the court is faced with naming a guardian when the parent nominated "Bob and Sue Jones," but Bob and Sue are no longer a couple. Now what? The court has to determine which of the two named people is more qualified, and the court may not make the decision you would have preferred.

You may want to argue with me here, certain in your belief that Bob and Sue will always be a couple. You could be right—Bob and Sue may never get divorced or legally separated—but what if one of them dies before you do? In many cases, you may find that the spouse of your number one choice wouldn't even be in the running for successor guardian. I hear this all the time:

Clients (confidently): We want to name Tom's brother Bob and his wife Sue as guardians.

Me: So if Bob can't act, then Sue should act alone?

Clients (exchanging horrified looks): Umm... No!!

Instead of naming both Bob and Sue, decide which of the two people you would choose if the couple weren't together and name that person individually. *Then* consider whether the remaining person would be your second choice if the first person couldn't act due to death or incapacity. If you name Bob individually as your first choice and then name someone other than Sue as your second choice, Sue will have no claim to guardianship if Bob can't act. On the other hand, if Sue really would be your next choice and you name her individually as successor to Bob, the court won't have to wonder what you would have wanted under the circumstances.

What if, after due consideration, you really do want to name Bob and Sue but only if they are still a couple at the time of your death? Perhaps Bob and Sue make a great team, but neither of them alone inspires the kind of confidence you are looking for in a guardian. Perhaps you believe very strongly in the necessity of a child being raised in a two-parent home. These feelings are understandable and it's certainly possible to specify that you are nominating a couple only if they are still together, but you should consider the consequences if life gets in the way of your plans.

I can't force you to go back and amend your list if you had any two-person designations in there, but I strongly suggest that you do so.

Narrow Down Your List - Factors to Consider

Now you need to figure out the very few parameters that are absolutely important to you and look for someone who fits those parameters adequately. Which parameters should you consider? That's an extremely personal question, and one that is impossible for me to answer. More important, the parameters you think are important can (and should) be tossed out the window if you have someone available who just feels right. Trust your gut on this one. That said, here are some points that you might want to consider:

- Religion. If you have a particular orientation toward religion (pro or con), you will probably be most comfortable selecting someone who shares that orientation. This approach dovetails nicely with what's best for your child—if your child has been raised to believe in a certain philosophy, he or she will feel more secure and less disrupted if that bedrock philosophy remains constant in the new surroundings. Let's say that your family is very active in a particular church; you attend services regularly and participate in church activities as often as possible. "Church" is part of your child's existence. Placing your child with a guardian who has no affiliation with any religious organization will effectively obliterate that part of your child's identity; even if the guardian is willing to take the child to services on Sundays, the child will know that "church" is not part of this new life, and the child will have to adjust to that. Any time you can reduce the number of adjustments that your child is going to have to face, you should.

- Parenting style. No matter whom you choose, your child will have to adjust to new house rules; every family approaches the intricacies of daily life in different ways. Again, however, the closer the guardian's parenting style matches your own, the less confusion and disruption your child will have to navigate. If you are relatively strict—established routines, clear expectations around what constitutes acceptable behavior, etc.—and you choose a guardian with a much more free-wheeling approach to life, your child may feel unsettled and confused as he or she learns to exist in the new (relatively) ruleless world. Conversely, if you think bedtime is just a suggestion and spontaneous road trips are wonderful, placing your child in a very structured household may make the child feel like he or she has been sentenced to prison.

- Location. Unless your child is very young, he or she likely has ties to your community that will be comforting as he or she adjusts to life without you. Maintaining friendships, attending familiar schools, and even going to favorite restaurants can provide a sense of continuity that will help your child through an enormously difficult time.

- Household circumstances. Does the prospective guardian have children already? Whether the answer is yes or no, consider how this will affect your child. Does the prospective guardian live in the city or country, and how will that affect your child? If your child has a pet, would the pet be welcome in the guardian's home? Especially if your child is on the older side, picture how he or she would fit into the prospective guardian's environment. An outdoors-oriented child likely would be happier with at least some room to roam, while a city kid might be completely adrift if moved to the "middle of nowhere."

- Existing relationship with your child. Sometimes the best choice on paper is someone you know well, but your child does not. Say you have a sister who lives a thousand miles away; you and she routinely keep in touch through emails and phone calls and you know her to be capable, loving, and philosophically compatible with you. She's financially stable and even has a house large enough to accommodate your child easily. She's part of the family so you know she would foster your child's relationships with grandparents, aunts and uncles, and cousins. In short, she's perfect.

But who is she to your child? Does the child know her well, or is she a somewhat abstract "Aunt Susie" that the child sees once a year or so at large family functions? To you, she's close family; to your child, she may effectively be a stranger. Luckily, this is one factor that's within your control: If you decide to designate Aunt Susie as guardian, you and she can make a concerted effort to let your child get to know Susie better as the child grows up. And if (as is extremely likely) you survive your child's childhood and Aunt Susie never has to assume the guardian role, your child will have benefited from your efforts anyway.

- Your child's wishes. This will not work for everyone, but if your child is of an age and mindset that allows him or her to contemplate your death without falling apart, ask him or her for input. I wouldn't suggest taking the input as an absolute directive, but a frank discussion with a (most likely older) child can be extremely helpful. After all, the child is the one most directly impacted by your decision. You may learn that your child has always been intimidated by Aunt Susie, but has always felt happy and comfortable around Uncle Rick—someone who hadn't even been on your radar screen before. You may learn that your child basically hates your community and would welcome the opportunity to start over somewhere else. In fact, depending on the child, you may find that your child has a better sense of who would be the best guardian than you do.

True story: A client related that when she was in fifth grade, she somehow found out who was named in her parents' Wills to act as her guardian. She said that although there was nothing objectively wrong with the prospective guardian, the thought of having to be raised by this woman was appalling. She had nightmares for weeks—not over the thought of her parents being dead, but over the thought of living with this particular guardian. I'm sure my client's parents would have wanted to know their daughter's feelings; it probably simply never occurred to them to ask.

- Willingness to act. In my experience, most clients hate to approach potential guardians; in fact, in my experience, many clients never do—they name who they name and never mention it to the designees. (I admit that I did the same thing once upon a time, so I'm certainly not in a position to criticize.) However, unpleasant as they may be, these discussions truly are valuable. Here's an innocuous opening to help you out:

"So, _____, we're in the process of drafting our Wills, and one of the hardest parts is deciding who would raise the kids if both of us went down in a plane crash or something. We would like to put you on our list of possibilities, but I wanted to know what you thought about it first. So... What do you think?"

You are likely to get one of three responses. First, the prospect may firmly and sincerely indicate his or her absolute willingness to be guardian. ("I would be honored to be named, and I promise I would do my best to raise your children right.") Second, the prospect may be hesitant but ultimately willing. ("Oh, wow, I don't even want to think about that. I don't know that I'm your best option, but of course I would step up if it came to that.") Third, the prospect may, for whatever reason, decline. ("You know I love you and the kids, but...") From what clients have told me, virtually all reactions fall into one of these three camps.

Review your list of prospects above and talk to each of them. If there is anyone on the list that you really don't want to contact, ask yourself why not: If you don't feel comfortable enough to talk to the person about being named guardian, how can you consider naming them? Go with your gut and remove that name from your list. If anyone you contact declines, remove that name from your list. People who hesitate may be perfectly acceptable choices—they may simply have been caught off guard—but take their reaction into consideration when you're making your final decision.

Now let's apply the above factors to your working list. Yes/no answers don't work particularly well in this instance since the factors are very subjective, so we'll use a 5-point scale with a 5 being absolutely out-of-the-park perfect and a 1 being completely deficient:

	#1	#2	#3	#4	#5
Religious compatibility?					
Similar parenting style?					
Same community?					
Household circumstances okay?					
Close to your child?					
Child approves?					
Willing to act?					
Total points					

Great, you have point totals—now what? Think about what the totals are saying about the relative merits of each prospect. Did anyone score significantly higher or lower than you would have expected? If so, does the score change your view about whether this person is a good choice? Now look at why the totals are what they are. Did one prospect score high because he nailed factors that aren't very important to you? If so, discount that high score as much as you feel is appropriate. The bottom-line numbers aren't meant to dictate your choices; they are meant to provide a framework for your thought process.

Your Final List

Once you have completed your analysis, restate your list of guardians in order of preference, leaving off anyone who no longer makes the cut.

Guardian

1) _____

2) _____

3) _____

Hooray! Another role filled.

Specifying People Who Shouldn't Act

Keep in mind that while you can nominate whomever you like to act as guardian, the court is not bound by your wishes—the court's job, always and forever, is to act in the best interests of the child. Sometimes this is a good thing; you may have named someone who can't or shouldn't or won't act when you die, and in that case you probably would be glad that the court isn't bound by your mistake. In other cases, though, you may want to give the court a heads-up about someone who is likely to request appointment as guardian but is someone whom you definitely do not want raising your child.

The way to accomplish this is by a brief and respectful but clear statement in your Will. Your attorney can determine how best to phrase your wishes from a legal perspective, but the statement may be something like "Although I love and respect my mother-in-law, Julie Kester, for reasons personal to me, it is my wish that she not be appointed as guardian of my minor children."

Is there someone (most likely a family member) who might press for appointment even if you have nominated someone else? Be sure to alert your attorney. Just so you don't forget, make a note here:

People who shouldn't be guardian even if they insist:

1) _____

2) _____

3) _____

Couples Who Can't Agree

Occasionally I run into couples who sincerely can't agree on who should be nominated as guardian. Since there is no legal requirement that both parents name the same individual(s), if you find yourself in this situation even after careful consideration and long discussion, go ahead and name whom you wish and let your spouse do the same—it's better than not having an estate plan at all. However, keep in mind that this makes order of death very important to your family (the spouse who dies last gets to name the guardian), so be sure to sleep with one eye open.

Trustee

A trustee's duties—managing finances and working with beneficiaries—are generally similar to an executor's duties, so sometimes the two roles get lumped together in people's minds. While there are certain similarities, when there is a trust, the trustee's role tends to be much more involved and last for a much longer period of time. For those reasons, you need to think particularly carefully about whom to name. (Hint: If you want to do anything but have all of your assets distributed free of strings when you die, you will need to name a trustee.)

What the Role Entails

Let's start with what a trustee does. As always, the particulars will depend on individual circumstances, but here are the typical responsibilities:

When the trust becomes active (for our purposes, when the trust creator dies):

- take control of all trust assets
- decide how the assets should be invested to achieve the overall objectives of the trust
- become familiar with the terms of the trust and the legal responsibilities they create
- meet with beneficiaries and become familiar with their individual circumstances
- retain an attorney, accountant, and (possibly) financial advisor
- open bank and brokerage accounts for the trust assets
- establish rules and routines around trust accounting and tax reporting
- oversee the preparation of the estate tax return and related returns
- fund various subtrusts as the trust agreement requires
- set up initial distribution schedules per the trust agreement

On an ongoing basis:

- monitor trust investments and change investment allocations as appropriate
- oversee the preparation of quarterly and/or annual income tax returns
- meet with beneficiaries periodically to review their circumstances
- determine whether adjustments should be made to distribution schedule
- address beneficiary requests for additional distributions for various purposes
- provide accountings to the trust beneficiaries

When the trust is ready to terminate:

- prepare the final distribution plan and have it approved by the beneficiaries (if appropriate)
- make arrangements for distributions
- file final tax returns
- formally terminate the trust

That's a long list, but it doesn't even include the heaviest burdens of being a trustee: Having responsibility for a family's financial well-being and acting as a counselor to the surviving spouse and (usually) the decedent's children.

This is not a job you want to assign to the first person who pops into your head.

Your Starter List

If you decided to work with a professional fiduciary in the Executor section, then your work is most likely done—simply name the same professional fiduciary to be the trustee (or co-trustee) of your trust and skip this section. Otherwise, grab your pen and, if you can, write down five people you know who would be capable of taking on the responsibilities outlined above:

Prospective trustee:

1) _____

2) _____

3) _____

4) _____

5) _____

Did you include any professional advisors on your list? It would make sense if you did; a financial advisor is going to know a lot about investments, for example, and an accountant would make easy work of those tax returns. However, if you did, think again: In many cases, these people are prohibited from acting as an independent trustee by the terms of their licenses, professional insurance, employment agreements, or rules of ethics governing their profession. If you have a legal, financial, or tax advisor on your list, you certainly can check with him or her to see whether appointment would be possible, but odds are you will need to replace that person with someone else.

Narrow Down Your List - Factors to Consider

Now let's winnow down your list by looking at some factors that make for a good trustee:

- Similar philosophy. In most cases, your trust document is going to give the trustee quite a bit of discretion. The trustee will have to decide whether "transportation" was meant to include a new sports car, whether "education" should include meditating somewhere in the Himalayas, whether training for the X Games counts as a "profession," etc. When selecting a trustee, you want to maximize the odds that the trustee will make the decision you would have wanted.

How do you know if a prospective trustee's general philosophy is similar to yours? Consider the individual's background, current lifestyle, and world view, as follows:

- Some people grow up privileged, some grow up "normal," and some grow up poor. For most people, the way they grow up has a profound effect upon how they view the world. (Think of the stereotypical "Depression baby" who reuses wrapping paper from last Christmas.) If you and your trustee grew up in similar circumstances, you are more likely to see eye-to-eye on how the trust should be managed.

- Current lifestyle also can be an important predictor of how well the trustee's decisions will mirror what you would have wanted. How do you feel if someone you care about asks you for $20? How about $100? $500? If you have limited means, $20 is a big deal; if you have unlimited means, $500 is couch change. Consider whether a prospective trustee's circumstances are so different from yours that it would impact his or her ability to carry out your intentions.

- "World view" is a broad term that includes opinions on the meaning and importance of work ethic, philanthropy, success, religion, family, and one's place in the world. Reasonable people can differ on these issues; I may think that success is measured by self-sufficiency and social status, while you may think that success is defined by the closeness of family and level of community service. If I were your trustee, I might encourage (or even push) your child to pursue a more lucrative career when you would have preferred that he pursue a less lucrative career with more of a "giving back" component. If you and your trustee share a similar world view, it is more likely that the trust funds will be used as you would have wanted.

(Side question: If you name a professional trustee, how do you know that the individual who manages your account will share your general philosophy? You don't. But rest assured that every trust officer I have ever known tries extremely hard to remove his personal views from the process and focus instead on whatever evidence he has of the trust creator's intent.)

- Ability to make unpopular decisions. If you're a parent, you know that your children will sometimes pull out all stops in an effort to get what they want. What if what your child wants is technically within the discretionary powers of the trustee to grant, but the trustee thinks it's a bad idea? Will the trustee have the fortitude to stick with the unpopular decision?

That may be an easy case—most of us have experience in saying no to children—but what if your surviving spouse wants a larger living allowance? The trustee may consider the request extravagant, but I can tell you from personal experience that it's hard to say no to an elderly widow(er). What if your surviving spouse wants a larger living allowance but is spending significant sums on a new flame, a new religious organization, or a new hobby (like gambling)? If your trustee doesn't have the wherewithal to stand firm, the security that the trust was meant to provide goes right out the window.

- Long-term commitment. If your trust assets will be distributed outright to the trust beneficiaries at or shortly after your death, then you are looking at a (relatively) short time frame. However, if the trust will continue for your spouse's lifetime and then even longer for your children's benefit, then you need to consider how long a prospective trustee will be able and willing to act. Depending on the terms of your trust, it may be extremely unlikely that any one person will serve as trustee for the entire trust term; still, you want someone who will be able to provide continuity at least for the first few years. Think not only of a prospective trustee's age, but also of how his or her life may change over the next few years—increasing job or family responsibilities, relocation, etc. Try to find someone who can provide your family with stable guidance for as long as possible.

If anyone on your list falls short based on these factors, seriously consider crossing them off.

Just as in the case of your guardian, you need to talk to your prospective trustees to see if they are willing to be named. Depending on the prospective trustee's background, this may be a more involved discussion; almost everyone has a general idea of what it means to be a guardian, but many people have no idea what it means to be a trustee. You will want to discuss the role in general and also discuss your goals and expectations. Feel free to emphasize that the trustee can seek assistance from professionals (at the expense of the trust) to complete necessary tasks, but listen carefully if your prospective trustee voices general discomfort at the idea of being named. A reluctant trustee can be a disaster.

Once you have talked to your prospects, it's time to compare them using the factors discussed above. Here's your chart:

	#1	#2	#3	#4	#5
Financially savvy?					
Similar philosophy?					
Ability to make unpopular decisions?					
Long-term commitment?					
Willing to act?					

Remember the Professional Fiduciary Option

If a professional fiduciary makes sense for the role of executor, it makes even more sense for the role of trustee. Consider the two special challenges of a trustee—detachment and longevity—and you may conclude that a professional simply can't be beat by an individual trustee. Yes, there are fees (usually approximately 1% per year), but professional management of a long-term trust is so important that the fees are usually well worth the services your beneficiaries receive.

What About Co-Trustees?

It's fairly common to name a surviving spouse as co-trustee of a revocable trust, and if it makes the spouse feel better to be involved, there's no particular reason not to do so. Naming an individual trustee to act in concert with a professional fiduciary can provide a sense of human contact for the family, especially if the individual trustee is a family member or a long-time friend. Naming two individuals to act as co-trustees can lead to confusion and needless difficulty unless the co-trustees work extremely well together; absent unusual circumstances, I wouldn't recommend it.

Your Final List

Finalize your list in light of your comparison. Most trust agreements empower an acting trustee to fill his or her own vacancy if no other successor is named, so if necessary you're probably safe with only two names. List your choices now:

Trustee:

1) _____

2) _____

3) _____

Attorneys-in-Fact (Agents)

You will need to make two designations with respect to your powers of attorney, one an attorney-in-fact for your financial matters (a "property agent") and the other an attorney-in-fact for your health care decisions (a "health care agent"). The qualities needed for each of these roles vary significantly, so you should avoid the temptation to name one person to act in both capacities simply because it's easier.

Property Agent

Your property power of attorney will give your agent control over your bank accounts, investment accounts, real estate—in essence, everything you own—if you no longer can or wish to exercise that control yourself at some point during your lifetime. If you become disabled, this person will pay your bills and figure out how to use your assets to maintain your lifestyle going forward. He or she will also decide how to fund your spouse's lifestyle if both of you were living on your assets.

It has been common practice for as long as I can remember for spouses to name each other as their property agent, with a back-up name or two following the spouse. I no longer think that this is *automatically* a good idea. In many (if not most) households, one spouse is in charge of keeping the household running—paying the bills, making or monitoring deposits, deciding whether a particular purchase is in budget or not, and so forth. If you are married and you're that person, then certainly it makes sense for your spouse to name you as his or her agent. However, if you're decidedly *not* that person, are you really going to have the wherewithal to deal with a disabled spouse and learn how to run household finances at the same time? The greater the disparity between the spouses (does your spouse know when your mortgage is due, or even which mortgage company holds the note?), the more I think you should consider leaving the non-involved spouse out of the equation and finding a better alternative.

What makes a good property agent? Someone who is organized, prudent, and accustomed to managing a household. Since your disability may trigger the appointment of a successor trustee if you have a revocable trust, and since both the property agent and the trustee need to have similar skills, it usually makes sense to name the same person for both roles—*if* you are naming an individual successor trustee. If your successor trustee is a professional fiduciary, you will want to check on their willingness to act as property agent (some will; some won't) and the fees for doing so.

For continuity's sake, it may make sense to name the same person for both the property agent and the executor roles, but it is not necessary. (Remember that the property agent is going to be acting *before* you die, while your executor only acts *after* you die.)

What about naming a child? If you are elderly and the child is already helping you manage your finances, then he or she probably is a good choice. However:

- If you have more than one child, consider how the move will be perceived by your other child(ren). A sour relationship between the named child and his or her sibling could prompt the non-named sibling to challenge the agent's actions just to cause trouble.

- In some families, the entire topic of finances is generally off-limits. Will you be comfortable baring your financial life to your child, or would you rather keep money out of the parent-child relationship? How does your child feel?

I don't mean to say that naming a child is always a mistake; the arrangement can work very well. But when it goes wrong, it tends to go very wrong—so tread carefully.

To summarize, only name your spouse as your first property agent if your spouse is already familiar with your household finances. If you have a trust and therefore have chosen a successor trustee, you will probably want to name that person to be your property agent should you need one. A good third (or second, if no spouse) back-up would be your executor, if different from your successor trustee. Name a child only if both you and the child are extremely comfortable with the arrangement. Beyond that, choose someone who is good at managing a household budget and has the time and commitment to take on the role. Make your list now:

Property agent:

1) _____

2) _____

3) _____

Health Care Agent

Your health care agent will make medical and quality-of-life decisions for you if you are unable to make or communicate them yourself. This could be as a result of an accident, a sudden medical incident such as a heart attack or stroke, or simply advancing age. Your health care agent will make any "pull the plug" decisions, but also will make less dramatic decisions such as whether you need to live in a care facility, and if so, which care facility is appropriate.

The factors to consider for this role are completely different from the factors for a property agent, an executor, or a trustee. Since the health care agent does not need to become involved in your financial affairs and since the decisions the agent will face are life decisions driven by psychology and philosophy, you want to look for someone with a very different skillset. (This is not to say that one person cannot be appropriate for both roles, but you shouldn't assume that they will be.) Factors to consider include:

- Commitment to you. The single most important factor to consider is whether the agent will carry out your wishes to the best of his or her ability regardless of any personal feelings or outside pressure to the contrary. You need someone who is strong enough to refuse extraordinary measures even if your family members vigorously disagree, if refusal is what you would have wanted. Conversely, if you have indicated that you want to be kept alive at all costs, you need someone who will fight for your life when you cannot do so yourself. It really doesn't matter if your agent shares your views on the "right" way to approach treatment; it is only important that he or she will follow your instructions no matter what.

- Ability to detach. Most people name one of their children as agent to serve if their spouse cannot do so. If you are going to name a child, select the one who will best be able to carry out his or her duties without suffering undue emotional damage. Most of my clients who have more than one child know without question which are the "sensitive" children and which are the "practical" children. Go for practical over sensitive.

- Willingness to act. Perhaps more so than any role other than guardian, you need to talk to your prospective health care agent and make sure that he or she is comfortable assuming this responsibility, especially if you want to refuse heroic medical measures at the end of your life. Some people—even people who would want those measures refused on their own behalf—do not want to be in a position to make life-or-death decisions for someone else, especially someone very close to them. Before making your final decisions, confirm that those you intend to name (including your spouse) are comfortable with the thought of carrying out your wishes.

- Availability. Sometimes decisions need to be made quickly. A good choice for health care agent need not live in your community, but he or she should be able to be reached without difficulty as a general rule. Mountain climbers, spies, people who refuse to carry a cell phone... Probably not your best choices.

Pen in hand? Make your list:

Health care agent:

1) _____

2) _____

3) _____

Congratulations! You have finished identifying the players who will be named in your estate plan. Go back now and review your choices; if you aren't satisfied (perhaps you have placed too much aggregate burden on one person or you have named people to work together who don't really get along), keep tinkering until you are. Once you're completely comfortable with your choices, you can move on to the next section.

Part Three:
Distribution Plan

Developing a distribution plan requires you to answer three questions. Relatively (perhaps deceptively) simple, these questions are:

1. What do I own?

2. Who gets what I own after I die? and

3. How and when do they get it?

What Do I Own?

The first question on our list may seem to be simple busy work, but it's not. In fact, of the 200 or so estates that I administered in a professional capacity, I would guess that only about 10% of them had asset lists that were anywhere close to complete at the time the decedent passed away. Most of the time the gaps and errors only served to make administration a bit more difficult, but occasionally the "what do I own?" question really came back to haunt us.

The whole purpose of this question is to save your executor and/or trustee the time, trouble, and expense of figuring out what you owned and addressing any sticky issues your assets may present. We won't be going into detail about the specific assets you own (bank account numbers and balances, real estate legal descriptions, etc.); we're more concerned with the *types* of assets you own and their ballpark value. At some point you may want to create a more comprehensive list for a couple of reasons:

- First, a complete list of your assets will be enormously helpful to your executor and will increase the odds that your estate will be settled quickly and completely the first time around. Some assets only leave a footprint once a year, and some don't even do that. There is nothing more frustrating than having to reopen an estate to deal with an asset that popped up after the estate was closed.

- Second, once you take the time to create a comprehensive list, it will be much easier to track changes in your net worth when you review your plan in the future (which you will, right?).

Figuring Out Your Net Worth

The is the most boring—at least to me—part of estate planning, but we need to get it out of the way before we continue. In order to make informed decisions about who gets what, you need to know what "what" is—the total value of the assets you will leave behind. Without at least a general idea of what you have to work with, you simply can't develop a clear picture of what your plan can and should accomplish.

First, write down a ballpark estimate of the current value of everything you own:

Home . . . . $ _____

Other real estate . . . . $ _____

IRAs . . . . $ _____

401(k)s . . . . $ _____

Other retirement accounts . . . . $ _____

Stocks/bonds/mutual funds . . . . $ _____

Checking and savings accounts . . . . $ _____

Life insurance (face value) . . . . $ _____

Business interests . . . . $ _____

Collections . . . . $ _____

Loans receivable (people owe you) . . . . $ _____

Installment contracts . . . . $ _____

Other . . . . $ _____

TOTAL TO THE GOOD . . . . $ _____

Now write down all of your debts:

Mortgages . . . . $ _____

Unsecured loans . . . . $ _____

Student loans . . . . $ _____

Credit card debt . . . . $ _____

Other . . . . $ _____

TOTAL TO THE BAD . . . . $ _____

Finally, subtract Total to the Bad from Total to the Good and write the result here:

MY NET WORTH . . . . $ _____

This number isn't precise and it certainly doesn't predict what your estate will be worth when you die, but it is good enough for our purposes. All we are trying to do is get an idea of the size of your sandbox.

Speaking of your sandbox, there may be some rocks and rusty cans hidden under the surface—some types of assets create issues that could make your estate more difficult to settle after you're gone and could fan the fires of family discontent unnecessarily. We're going to deal with those issues now.

Untitled Assets

By definition, you are only allowed to direct the disposition of assets you actually owned at the time of your death. "Owned" is easily determined if an asset has some sort of process for identifying title (bank accounts, real estate, automobiles, etc.). However, some assets have no such process associated with them; these include most items of personal property such as jewelry, antiques, coins, artwork, and other collectibles. In these cases, you need to stake your claim (or, conversely, deny your claim) clearly while you are alive.

Let's say you own a very expensive painting (we'll make it a Rembrandt). There is no central registry for art ownership, so the only real "proof" of ownership is, frankly, circumstantial. Your grandfather bought the Rembrandt from a dealer; he gave it to your mother, who gave it to you. Or did she? After your death, what if your ne'er-do-well brother pops up and claims that Mom gave the painting to him and he was just letting you store it in your house? What if there is no one around who can conclusively rebut his claim? Even if you bought the Rembrandt yourself and there is a receipt to prove it, someone (maybe one of your heirs; maybe not) may claim that you gave or sold the painting to him or her before your death. And without you there to deny the claim, the question of ownership may have to be decided by the court, and it may not be decided correctly.

If you are in possession of untitled assets when you die, they likely will be presumed to be yours unless someone claims otherwise; if that happens, your executor or a probate judge is going to have to settle the claim. If the asset truly isn't yours—you have only borrowed it or you're storing it for someone else—avoid unnecessary strife by explaining the situation here:

I am in possession of the following assets on a long-term basis, but I do not own them:

1) _____

2) _____

3) _____

Loans to children

Okay, most of us don't have a Rembrandt hanging around, but here's something that many of us *do* have, and it's a frequent cause of contention: Loans to children. If you have ever helped out one of your children financially, you need to clarify the transaction. Did you mean it to be a gift? If you meant it to be a loan, what were the terms? Was it (or any part of it) paid off? If you don't clarify these things before you die, you leave open the possibility of disagreements among your children, possibly rising to the level of a court action.

Loans to children are so common that we're going to document them right now. Grab your pen and fill out the following:

_____ I have made no loan to any of my children that I expect the child to repay.

_____ I have made repayable loans to my children as follows:

Child	Amount	Terms of repayment
_____	_____	_____
_____	_____	_____
_____	_____	_____

You don't have to get all legal when you fill out "terms of repayment" above; you just want to make a note of the general understanding. Phrases like "being repaid now" or "to be offset against inheritance if still unpaid" will suffice. All you really need to do at this point is clarify that the amount you gave to the child was a loan, not a gift.

Orphan assets

Orphan assets are those things that have no real economic or sentimental value but can't be disposed of easily. For people of my parents' generation, the classic orphan asset is a vacant piece of land somewhere in Florida that was supposed to be in the path of future development. They bought it as an investment when they were young parents, they have paid the nominal property taxes annually ever since, they still own it, it's still vacant, and it probably will be vacant until the end of time. When they die, if they have three children and a typical equal-among-children estate distribution pattern, then each of the three children will be the proud owner of a one-third interest in a nearly-worthless vacant lot in Florida. Don't ask me how I know.

If you have one of these orphan assets—vacant land, minor partnership interest, unattractive timeshare arrangement—do everyone a favor and get rid of it now. It's far easier for you to dispose of this property than it will be for your beneficiaries to dispose of it after you're gone.

How can you get rid of orphan assets? The best option is to sell them, if a market exists at all. Try going back to the person or entity that sold you the asset in the first place; perhaps they will know of a potential buyer or even will be willing to buy the asset back themselves. Don't expect to be pleasantly surprised by the asset's value—remember, your goal here is to get rid of the asset, not to make a fortune on the deal.

If there truly is no way to sell the asset, then consider donating it to charity, if possible. Many charities won't want your asset any more than your heirs would, but some smaller charities may be grateful for any donation and will be willing to take on your problem child.

If you can't sell it and you can't give it away, you may want to consider abandoning the asset. If it's a piece of real estate, for example, simply stop paying the annual real estate taxes. Eventually the taxing entity will hold a tax sale and your problem will be solved. Any asset that carries a periodic fee of some sort (taxes, membership fees, maintenance fees, etc.) probably can be disposed of in this manner.

Finally, if you can't do any of the above, the least you can do is leave the property to a single individual. Dividing it among multiple beneficiaries (such as your children) only makes disposing of it more difficult after you're gone.

Make a list of your orphan assets now and commit to deal with them before your estate planning documents are finalized. (Note: Do not consider this an excuse to put off finalizing your documents!) Simplify your life and the lives of your executor and beneficiaries; you'll feel good as a result.

I will sell (or try to sell) these assets:

1) _____

2) _____

3) _____

I will give away these assets:

1) _____

2) _____

3) _____

I will abandon these assets:

1) _____

2) _____

3) _____

Collections

Five words that will strike fear in any seasoned executor: *Dad had a coin collection.* Not because coin (or similar) collections are difficult to administer *per se*, but because you are absolutely guaranteed to hear these nine words next: *and some of the coins are really worth something.*

Um, no, they're not. What's in that box is almost certainly the same assortment of coins (or stamps, or election memorabilia, or you name it) as in a million similar boxes in a million similar households.

If you have personal property that you have ever even suggested is "worth something," do everyone a favor and get it appraised before you die. Why? As always, it's to minimize the potential for argument. If your executor obtains an appraisal of your collection after your death that shows a value of $800, not the $8,000 or $80,000 or more that everyone expected, the appraisal—and the executor—will be eyed with suspicion (or worse) by the beneficiaries. If *you* have obtained an appraisal that shows a value of $800 and tucked the appraisal in with the collection, the beneficiaries won't bat an eye. Your endorsement of the appraisal will completely defuse a potentially difficult situation.

True story: I once administered an estate that included a diamond. It was about a carat, if I remember correctly, and depending on whom you wanted to believe, it was either a practically worthless diamond of very poor color and quality or it was an exotic "yellow" diamond of incredible value. The certified gemologist who appraised it was of the former opinion; the decedent's child was quite firmly of the latter opinion. Three additional appraisals later, the child finally was persuaded to back off of a threatened lawsuit against us for refusing to acknowledge the diamond's "true" value. I firmly believe that all of this could have been avoided if the decedent had obtained an appraisal during his lifetime.

Of course, it is possible that you really *do* have a valuable collection, or at least a valuable collectible or two. If that's the case, it's even more important to get it appraised and keep the appraisal with your estate planning documents. It's a lot of work to clear out a household after someone's death, and regardless of the diligence of an executor it's possible that something of significant value might get lost in the shuffle. Help your executor out by alerting him or her to special items that could otherwise be overlooked. Do it here:

I own the following items of personal property which I believe may have significant value:

1) _____

2) _____

3) _____

4) _____

5) _____

Who Gets My Stuff?

Now comes the fun part—deciding who will get your stuff when you die. There are three steps to this process. First, you will figure out who gets your personal property and how the property will be divided among them. Second, you will decide whether you want to leave specific amounts of money to anyone. Finally, you will decide who will benefit from everything else—the "residue" of your estate.

Personal Property

"Personal property" means household furnishings, automobiles, clothing, books, stamp collections—basically everything tangible other than money, investments, and real estate. Personal property is not likely to be worth much, relatively speaking, but in at least some families the disposition of personal property is more likely than anything else to raise issues.

Why all the drama? I believe there are three primary reasons, and it is good to keep them in mind as you consider what to do with your personal property. First, if there are going to be emotional issues, they are likely to arise around these personal items rather than around a stock certificate or bank account. Second, the concept of "value" kind of goes out the window when you're dealing with personal items, and the uncertainty created by the inability to value items with any certainty can make people uncomfortable—crazy, even. Third, unlike many other assets, a personal item usually cannot be divided among more than one potential recipient.

- Emotional issues arise in connection with personal property because those items form the framework of our memories. A cookie jar, a hand-crocheted blanket, an often-worn necklace, a favorite children's book—these are the things that connect us to our past and provide a tangible reminder of our family roots. When a loved one (often a parent) has just died, we naturally want to save physical reminders of what we have lost. So what happens when a particularly important reminder is scooped up by someone else?

What happens is the classic family rift that everyone wants to avoid. That old electric train set that sat in the attic forgotten for thirty years? Its disposition to one person instead of another becomes proof positive (in the other's eyes) that:

- Mom and Dad always liked you better;

- You always get what you want, you spoiled brat; and

- Once again, I get the short end of the stick.

There are few events in life more stressful and emotional than the death of a parent, and even children who generally get along may find old wounds bursting open without a Band-Aid in sight. In the heat of the moment, hateful things are said; those things are hard to take back. It can take years for a family to put itself back together once it's been ripped apart.

- Directing that personal property be divided "equally" doesn't always avoid family issues because "equal" implies that there is a foolproof way to quantify and assign value to the items. There is not. If I get Mom's jewelry, books, and car while my brother gets the stamp collection, family tools, and grandfather clock, are we even? An appraisal may say yes, but I (and/or my brother) may say no.

- Some items (a silver tea service or a set of china, for example) may be worth much more as a complete set than as individual pieces, making them more difficult to distribute equally and fairly. If these items represent a large part of the appraised value of the personal property, a problem arises. I have worked on several "ordinary" estates in which the personal property consisted of a houseful of used furniture, a ten-year-old auto, a smattering of jewelry... and Great-Grandma's heirloom china. If one child gets the china, the other (let's say) three children feel gypped—and economically speaking, they are. If the china is split among the four children, each gets a nearly-useless gift of three place settings. Sell the family heirloom and split the proceeds? Ouch.

In a perfect world, your Will could simply direct everyone close to you to take what they want of your personal property and then sell or donate what's left over. You can do that—it's your right—but if you want to help your survivors (and your executor) avoid needless pain, you should consider doing more. Here are some approaches that I've seen and what I think of them; as you read through the options, add your own thoughts and reactions:

- List specific items in your Will. If you have a small number of items whose disposition is very important to you, you can refer to them specifically in your Will (e.g., I give my Super

Bowl ring to my son Bob). This is the most sure-fire way to guarantee that the item goes to the right person; your executor is legally bound to deliver the item and it would take a Will contest to thwart your wishes. On the down side, if you change your mind in the future, it will take a formal codicil (amendment) to your Will to change the distribution.

Are there any specific items that you definitely want to include in your Will? If so, list them here, along with their intended recipients:

Item	Recipient

- Leave a list. It is a fairly common practice to include a clause in your Will that refers to a separate list of items of personal property and their intended recipients. This list can be as long or as short as you wish and can be changed as often as you wish before your death. (Be sure to date the new list and destroy the prior list each time you prepare an update.) The list should be specific enough to avoid ambiguity and should be updated if an item on the list is sold or given away.

The benefit of this approach is its ease of use. You can take as long as you want to make your list, and you can change it whenever you see fit. The drawback to this approach is that with no one to force you to make the list and keep it up to date, the odds of you doing so are not good. Most people who take this approach may as well not have bothered.

Be honest: Do you think you would follow through on making your list and keeping it up to date?

_____ Yes _____ No _____ Possibly

- Put names on items. What I am referring to here is the practice of writing names on small stickers and attaching the stickers to the items the named recipient is supposed to get. I have heard of a twist on this practice in which sticker "dots" of different colors are used, with a master list somewhere that indicates who is meant by which color.

Please don't do this. It is a horrible idea.

First, don't think for a second that your children won't spend the next few holiday gatherings surreptitiously checking behind paintings and underneath furniture to see who's getting what. This may give them something to do, but surely there are better family activities to be pursued.

Second, don't think for a second that the adhesive on those stickers is fail-safe; stickers will eventually simply fall off and get lost, leaving the distribution of those items up in the air. Finding a wayward sticker on the floor is worse than you can imagine, because now everyone knows that Cousin Susie was supposed to get *something*, but no one knows what she was supposed to get.

Third, don't think for a second that everyone in your family is above switching or replacing stickers to get what they want, up to and including nearly everything. I have seen it happen. (Okay, I haven't *seen* it happen, but it has been reported to me by a disgruntled beneficiary more than once.)

The sticker-on-item approach seems to have died down after enjoying a swell in popularity during the late 1980s, but it could rear its ugly head at any time. Don't succumb. Sign this pledge:

I promise that I will not use the sticker-on-item approach even if everyone else is doing it.

Sign here: _____

- Sell everything. Your Will can direct the sale of all of your personal property, with the proceeds to be added to the residue of your estate and distributed accordingly. This is what will happen anyway to items that no one wants, but including a directive in your Will that everything be sold eliminates any legal leeway your executor may have exercised in terms of getting your property to those who will cherish it the most. I include it as an option here in the spirit of full disclosure, but please don't do it.

True story: I had a client who had been through such an ordeal when his parents died that he directed his executor to sell all of his possessions—every single thing, no exceptions—when he died and split the cash proceeds evenly among his children. This struck me as a bad idea, but he was insistent. I am hopeful that when the time comes, his executor will turn a blind eye and let the children remove items of sentimental value; I hate to think of a family's history being lost in this manner.

True story update: Just had another one. People seem to be so afraid of family strife after their death that they are willing to trash a lifetime of memories in order to avoid it. I truly hope you can find a better way.

- Let people take turns. This is a creative approach, and I have seen it work well. Once the personal property has been appraised, the group of recipients (usually the decedent's children, but it could be any defined group) draw lots to determine a selection order. (Think pulling numbers out of a hat.) Selector #1 then picks any one thing that he or she wants. Selector #2 does the same, followed by #3, and so on until everyone has picked one item. Selector #1 then goes again, and this process continues until everything that anyone wants has been assigned. Everything that's left gets sold or donated.

The beauty of this approach is that each person is able to select what's most important to him or her without battling anyone else for it. If it's available when your turn comes, you can take it. Unless there are only one or two extremely valuable items, the overall division should be fairly equal; if it's not, it's because people chose what they wanted without regard to cash value—which is as it should be. Logistics can make this approach problematical, but "virtual" divisions are possible. Overall, while disagreements can still occur, this approach tends to deliver the best result for everyone.

Does this sound like it might work for your family? ___ Yes ___ No ___ Maybe

- Hold a family auction. I have seen this one work beautifully, and I have seen it turn into a fiasco. Each member of the group of recipients is credited with an amount of "play money" which can be used to bid on items of interest; the more important an item is to someone, the more he or she will bid. In theory, everyone will walk away with what they wanted the most within the bounds of fairness.

True story #1: I was administering the estate of the mother of a set of four delightful children, three children-in-law, and a handful of youngish grandchildren. The mother had not specified how to divide the personal property other than to say that it should be distributed in "relatively equal shares" among the children. (That's a pretty common clause.) The kids themselves decided to take the auction approach. Each child was assigned a bankroll which he or she then shared with his or her spouse and children as he or she saw fit. The auction itself felt like a party; there was plenty of good-natured competitiveness and many stories were shared as items came up for bid. No one walked away from the process feeling anything but satisfied.

True story #2: Same general situation as #1, except that the heirs were quite a bit less delightful and the auction concept was specified in the instructions referenced in the Will, so no one had a choice. These heirs didn't like each other much and the competitiveness was real and ugly. No one walked away happy, but that probably had much more to do with the players than with the game.

How does this option feel to you?

_____ It makes sense.

_____ I think my family would enjoy participating.

_____ I think my family would hate this idea.

_____ It's too complicated.

_____ I don't care; I'll be dead.

- Talk it out. If you find yourself with one item of significant value (like Great-Grandma's china) and several potential takers (like those four children), work out the disposition of that item while you are still alive. You may find that some of your beneficiaries are perfectly willing to let the item go to someone else, and that's an important thing to know. Perhaps the others can agree on a plan to share the item that will satisfy everyone. You'll never know until you ask.

- Give it away now. If you are elderly and in possession of a lifetime of personal property acquisitions, it's likely that many of them are sitting in a drawer somewhere, rarely if ever used. If that's the case, why wait until your death to give these items to people who will love and use them? Instead of buying gifts for your loved ones on typical gift-giving holidays, give them something from your past along with a note about the item's history. I guarantee they will appreciate this gift much more than anything new you could buy for them. (True story: Thanks, Mom.)

Which of the above approaches is right for you? It really depends on your property, your family, and your views on the importance of both. You may change your mind over time, but for now simply complete the following items and we'll move on:

I know that I want to leave the following items to the people indicated:

Item	Recipient
_____	_____
_____	_____
_____	_____
_____	_____
_____	_____

Other than the items noted above, I _____ do _____ don't care what happens to my personal property.

Other than the items noted above, I want to limit distribution of my personal property to the following people (write "don't care" if you don't care):

_____

_____

My Will should direct distribution according to the following method:

_____ I will leave a list of specific items; everything else should be distributed as noted below.

_____ Give my property in roughly equal shares to the people listed above; let my executor decide the specifics.

_____ Let the people listed above take what they want however they want and sell or donate the rest.

_____ Use the "take turns" approach outlined above.

_____ Use the "auction" approach outlined above.

_____ Sell everything and add the sale proceeds to my residuary estate.

_____ Let my personal property flow along with my residuary estate; let my executor/trustee decide what to do with it.

I need to talk to my beneficiaries about the dispositions of these items:

_____

_____

_____

_____

One last suggestion before we move on: *Please* talk to your family members about what items are most important to them before you finalize your plan. I talk with people about estate planning a lot (obviously), and almost every one of those people has one thing, usually something small and of no significant value, that they either a) hope with all their heart they will receive when their loved one dies, or b) regret with all their heart that they did not receive when their loved one died. Often the item in question is so small and ostensibly insignificant that no one would ever guess its meaning to the person who treasures it—and if that's the case, then what are the odds it will end up going to the right person? Slim. The item gets thrown into a box of miscellany and given to someone who doesn't want it, or it gets sold at a garage sale, or it gets donated along with a lot of other minor items to a local charity, or it simply gets tossed in the trash. And that, my friend, is a tragedy.

Ask each of your loved ones if there is any one thing of yours that they especially want to receive when you die. If there is, and if it doesn't disrupt your overall plan, try to make sure that the item gets to the one who will cherish it the most.

Specific Monetary Bequests

You have the ability in your Will to leave specific items or specific amounts of money to certain people however you wish—as long as you own it, you can give it away. We have already discussed how to leave specific items of property to intended beneficiaries; therefore, this section only deals with monetary bequests (such as "I leave $1000 to my first grade teacher, Miss Anderson").

Specific bequests of money make sense when you want to do something for someone (or for a charity) but you don't want them to share in the residue of your estate. A specific bequest will be paid first, so be judicious with your bequests—you don't want to inadvertently leave your residuary beneficiaries with nothing! In fact, it's a good idea to compare the total of any specific bequests to your net worth from time to time, making sure that the bequests are still in line with your overall wishes.

Remember that you don't *have* to leave monetary bequests to anyone (in fact, most people don't), but if you want to, write down the recipients here, along with your initial feeling as to what amounts would be appropriate. You may want to adjust the amounts later as the plan for your residue takes shape.

Recipient	Amount
_____	_____
_____	_____
_____	_____
_____	_____
_____	_____

Residue

Now comes the fun part, at least for most people. You've disposed of your personal property, you have (or have not) provided for specific bequests, and now you're faced with how to dispose of everything else—called the residue of your estate. The good news is that the law allows you to do almost anything you want; the bad news is that this flexibility, coupled with an inherent uncertainty as to what the future will look like, can make decision-making exceedingly difficult.

What You Can't Do

While it is true that the law allows you to do almost anything you want with your residue, there are limits. Let's get them out of the way now.

- Completely disinherit your spouse. If you are legally married at the time of your death, your spouse is entitled to some portion of your estate regardless of your wishes. The amount to which a spouse is entitled varies by state but it is never nothing. Note that a spouse is entitled to a portion of your estate even if you have been separated for many years and even if your marriage is in the process of being terminated. Also note that in a few states, you can be legally married and not even know it—acting like you're married in certain specific ways can create a "common law" marriage that is legally identical to a traditional license-and-ceremony marriage. Needless to say, if you're not sure if you're married, you might want to consult an attorney.

- Set conditions that are against public policy. You can't force someone to do something illegal in order to receive a portion of your estate; if you try, the provision will be nullified. You also can't violate public policy by linking an inheritance to a violation of someone's civil rights. Your attorney will let you know if your planned distribution scheme runs afoul of this rule.

- Tie up your funds forever. You can establish a trust that will be in existence for a mighty long time, but there has to be an end point. I won't go into details (ask your lawyer friends about the "rule against perpetuities" and watch them tremble); it's enough for you to know that at some point you just have to let go.

And that's about it as far as limitations go. In almost every other case, even if what you do is nonsensical or ludicrous, the court will try to find a way to figure out what you wanted and make it work as well as possible. If you leave money to your pet (animal rights aside, pets can't own property), the court will interpret that to mean that you wanted your pet to be cared for, and will impose a trust for the pet's benefit. If you leave your money to "charity," the court will look for evidence of what charities were important to you and get the money to them. People often talk about the danger of your assets going to "the state," but the reality is that a probate court will go to great lengths to avoid that result.

Create Your Plan

The obvious first step in creating your distribution plan is to decide who will be involved—the beneficiaries of your residuary estate. The key here is to keep at it until you have provided for most potential scenarios, and that's not as easy as it sounds.

I have been an estate planning attorney for a number of years and have drafted a whole lot of Wills and trusts. This is my least favorite conversation, one which played itself out far too often:

Me: So, Mr. and Mrs. Client, how do you want your assets distributed when you die?

Mr. Client, confidently: To each other, of course.

Me: Okay, and what happens when you're both gone?

Mr. Client, less confidently: Well, um, then, to our children, if we have any.

Me: Certainly. And if not?

Mr. Client, fumbling: Then, um, I guess to charity. [Looking at Mrs. Client.] Maybe the Heart Association?

Mrs. Client: Or maybe the Art Institute. We both like art.

Mr. Client: Good point. The Art Institute sounds good. [Looking at me.] What do you think?

What do I think? I think Mr. and Mrs. Client have more work to do before we can even think about drafting their documents. I am not them—chances are I don't even know them very well, if at all—and I have no business making these decisions for them. They need to make the "what if?" decisions for themselves.

Why bother? Frankly, most people lose interest in thinking about beneficiaries once they get beyond their immediate family (usually spouse and children, or for single people, parents and siblings). This is understandable—the odds are good that you will not be the last of your immediate family to die, so further planning can seem like a pointless exercise—but I challenge you to do better. Unforeseen events can happen; the unlikely is not impossible. Your worldly wealth, large or small, has to go somewhere. It's up to you to direct its disposition. Read on:

A Tribute to Robert Walsh

True story, and this might be my favorite story of all. I hope it makes you smile and also spurs you to think deeply about how to "spend" your money when you're gone.

Robert Walsh was one of the first estates I was given when I became an estate administrator back in the early 1990s. He had named our local bank as administrator in his estate planning documents, but beyond that, no one knew much about him. He had never had any significant contact with the bank, his attorney didn't remember much about him, and the people who worked in the nursing home where he lived the last few years of his life could only say that he kept pretty much to himself. No known family, no real visitors, nothing but an old man—he was 95 years old when he died—who stayed in his room and didn't bother anyone.

As I went through his belongings (part of my job), I was able to piece together at least an outline of Mr. Walsh's life. His father made knives, a valuable trade in the late 1890s, and he was recruited to come to America from England by a well-known knife-maker. The Walshes moved around a fair amount when Robert was young—from New York State to the small town of Fremont, Ohio to other small towns in the Midwest, ultimately landing in Evanston, Illinois. Robert grew up and married a woman named Katherine, who died in the 1960s. They never had children. They were both only children themselves. Even their parents were only children. At the time of his death, Mr. Walsh had no known living relatives (the first and only time I ever saw that) and no close friends. He had outlived everyone.

But he hadn't outlived the town of Fremont, Ohio, to which he left his entire estate. Under the terms of his trust, all of his assets were to be liquidated, with the proceeds given to Fremont to be used to "enhance and beautify the lives of its citizens." All told, his assets amounted to somewhere around eight hundred thousand dollars.

As luck would have it, I was planning a weekend trip to see family in Toledo, Ohio, not terribly far from Fremont. I decided to go a day early, visit Fremont, and tell the mayor about the bequest in person. I really wasn't sure what to expect—was eight hundred thousand dollars a lot of money to a city, or was it a blip on the radar? Would the mayor even care? Would Mr. Walsh's bequest make any difference at all?

The mayor was a genial Midwestern guy, probably not a whole lot older than me. He welcomed me into his office and we chatted a while before we got down to business. I explained that my employer was administering Mr. Walsh's estate and that Fremont was the beneficiary; I explained the process that we would go through and how long it would take. He listened attentively but as I droned on, I could see the big question bubbling up and trying to find a polite way to get out of his mouth. Midwestern people are like that.

Finally, he couldn't help himself. "If I could ask," he started, "are we talking about a *little* bit of money, or... more than a little? Do you have any idea?"

I hemmed and hawed for a minute, saying that the administration wasn't complete and so a precise figure wasn't possible, blah, blah, blah, and then I spilled it. "When all is said and done, we should be looking at around eight hundred thousand." Pause. "Give or take."

His jaw dropped, just like in cartoons. I had never seen a reaction like that in real life. "Dollars?" he finally said. "Eight hundred thousand dollars?"

I confirmed that yes, it would be around eight hundred thousand dollars, maybe a little more or less but probably close.

He sat there for a minute, and then his eyes misted up, and he started talking—slowly at first, then more and more animated as reality sank in. He told me the sad state that Fremont was in, told me of plant closings and unemployment and a general feeling that the town was dying. He had just that morning been to one of the few remaining major employers in Fremont; he had to deliver the news that the plant was being shut down for environmental reasons. It was going to be a major blow to the citizens of the town, but now he had something good to help counterbalance the bad news.

As he talked, an idea formed in his mind: Fremont owned a piece of land on the river, but there had never been funds to do anything with it. Now there were. He talked of using the Walsh gift as a starting point to get matching funds and grants and whatever else they could find, and turn the land into a beautiful park. With a communal building where people could have picnics and family reunions, he ventured. And hiking trails. And a garden. And maybe even a swimming pool. Suddenly this man had a mission and he wanted to get started, so I left.

About a year later, I got an invitation to the Fourth of July dedication of the Robert L. Walsh Park in Fremont, Ohio. The invitation promised a parade, a dedication ceremony, and a picnic for the entire town. It was straight out of a Frank Capra movie. I couldn't go, but thanks to the internet I've been able to check in on Fremont and Walsh Park from time to time over the years. The park is still there, the largest in Fremont, and it is still enhancing and beautifying the lives of everyone who uses it. I hope that somehow Mr. Walsh knows what he accomplished.

When it comes to estate planning, most Americans are pretty uncreative. I think in part this is because what little exposure most people have to estate planning is, almost without exception, based on a single picture of human life—a married couple with children. Everything goes to the spouse, then to the children. That's just how we roll.

But what if you're not married, or you have no children, or you and your children are estranged? Then you end up in an attorney's office with no real idea what's possible, much less what you might want to do with your stuff. That's not the basis of a solid estate plan, but to some extent it's really not your fault. This section of the guide is designed to help.

In all honesty, you may not need to complete this section in the detail that it appears to require. You may have a very clear picture already of where you want your residue to go; perhaps you have a large happy family to support or you have a single cause to which you have devoted your life and to which you wish to devote your assets when you die. If that's the case—if you already know exactly where your residue is to go—then feel free to breeze through this section and emerge at the end with the list you already knew you would make. The detailed steps that follow are meant to assist those who aren't sure (or have never even considered) what they want to do.

To make the following process less confusing, you are going to walk through it with two fictional characters—"Pat," who is married with three children, and "Chris," who is single and childless. Obviously you don't need to make the same decisions as Pat or Chris, but seeing how they approach and complete each step may help you in your decision-making process.

Step One: Consider the Possibilities

We'll start with a list of types of beneficiaries to get you thinking about what you want. We will then use this information to construct your distribution plan. Go through the list below and mark how you feel about each entry—yes (you definitely want to include as a residuary beneficiary), no (not interested or not applicable), or maybe (you may want to include as a back-up residuary beneficiary if you run out of other ideas).

Yes	No	Maybe	
			Spouse/Partner
			Child(ren)
			Grandchild(ren)
			Parent(s)
			Sibling(s)
			Niece(s)/Nephew(s)
			Aunt(s)/Uncle(s)
			Cousin(s)
			Friend(s)
			Caretaker(s)
			Church
			Charity - education
			Charity - medical research
			Charity - aid for underprivileged
			Charity - religious
			Charity - animals
			Charity - political
			Charity - environmental
			Charity - civic organization
			Charity - other

Now summarize your list by writing all of your "yes" beneficiaries here by name (e.g., if you marked "Niece(s)/nephew(s)" to indicate a desire to include your nephew Jimmy, put "Jimmy" here):

1) _____

2) _____

3) _____

4) _____

5) _____

6) _____

7) _____

8) _____

9) _____

10) _____

Step Two: Refine Your List

Look at the list above in the cold light of your net worth and consider whether the list is realistic. Unless you have a very small list or a very large net worth, refine the list as follows:

1) For those you included as a token of respect or affection rather than out of a desire to provide support, consider adding them to your specific bequest list and removing them from your residuary beneficiary list.

Example: You included your father's caretaker, who has become almost a part of the family. You don't mean to provide her with ongoing support or give her a significant share of your residue; you just want to do something nice for her to remind her that she was loved and appreciated. You decide that a specific bequest of a few thousand dollars will do the trick.

2) Rearrange the names in order of importance from high to low.

3) If there are names on the list who should benefit only if all higher-priority needs have been met (call them the "B" list), place an asterisk next to them.

Example: Your list includes family members from a lower generation (e.g., grandchildren) who should receive funds only if those in a higher generation (e.g., children) don't survive you or don't need support.

4) Group all asterisked names at the bottom of the list.

Here's how Pat and Chris completed this step:

Pat: Wow, I have too many beneficiaries here. All I really care about is my spouse Lee and our three kids, although I really would like to leave *something* to the ASPCA—that's very important to me—and I promised Mom and Dad before they died that I would always look after my disabled sister Beth as best I could. I can't even consider going back on that promise. I think I'll add the ASPCA to my specific bequest list instead of including it here, make Lee, Beth, and my kids "A" beneficiaries, and make everyone else "B" beneficiaries. So here's my refined list:

1) Lee

2) Beth

3) Kids

4) Friends*

5) University*

Chris: I really want to help out the whole world but some people are more important to me than others. My brother does okay for himself, but he'll never be able to send my nieces to college—I want to do that. Looking at my net worth, I think I can cover the college expenses with about half of my funds. The rest I'll divide between my best friend Mike and my cousin Loretta. If my nieces don't need all of their funds for college, the leftovers can go to my local community foundation. I think everyone else will just have to get along without me. So here's my refined list:

1) Nieces

2) Mike

3) Loretta

4) Community Foundation

Rewrite your refined list here:

1) _____

2) _____

3) _____

4) _____

5) _____

6) _____

7) _____

8) _____

9) _____

10) _____

Step Three: Timing

You should now have a group of "A" beneficiaries and (perhaps) a group of "B" beneficiaries with asterisks by their names. Think about the "A" (non-asterisked) beneficiaries first. Do you mean for all of them to start benefiting from your estate as soon as you die, or should some wait until later?

Example: The church should get its distribution only after your spouse dies, or your siblings should get their share only after your parents are gone.

If you want to include timing like this in your distribution plan, make appropriate notes on your revised list. For example, after "American Heart Association," you might write "after my Aunt Susie dies." When you have finished, put your "A" beneficiaries in chronological order, with the initial beneficiaries first and subsequent beneficiaries next.

Pat says: My spouse Lee comes before the kids; they should only get what's left over after Lee dies. So my initial beneficiaries will be Lee and my sister Beth. Here's my list:

Initial: Lee, Beth

Subsequent: Children, after Lee dies

Chris says: I want to set aside the college funds for my nieces from the start, even though they won't actually use the money for a few years. Mike and Loretta don't really *need* anything from me; I could just put it all into the college fund and give Mike and Loretta their distributions when the girls are done with school. Then again, why should they wait? No, I'll make the college fund, Mike, and Loretta the initial beneficiaries and list the community foundation as a subsequent beneficiary, since it won't get anything until the girls are out of college.

Initial: College fund for nieces, Mike, Loretta

Subsequent: Community foundation, after the girls are out of school

Your turn: List your "A" beneficiaries in chronological order:

Initial:

_____

_____

_____

_____

_____

Subsequent:

_____

_____

_____

_____

_____

Step Four: Dividing the Pot

If you have more than one initial beneficiary, you need to decide how access to the residuary assets should be handled. Will all of your initial beneficiaries share the residue equally? If not, who gets more and who gets less? Do you want to split your residue into shares right away, or should everyone have access to the entire residue on an as-needed basis until some point in time?

Pat's answer: The issue is how much Lee's trust should get and how much Beth's trust should get. I could think about it one of two ways: Allocate as much as I think Lee will need to Lee's share and then let whatever is left over be Beth's share, or vice versa. Either way, I may leave one of them with too much or too little—it's so hard to predict the future. Maybe what I should do is just leave my entire residue as one big pot and let the trustee make distributions to Lee and Beth based on their needs over time. Yeah, that's it.

Chris's answer: I already decided that half of my residue should be enough to take care of the college expenses, so that leaves the other half for Mike and Loretta. There's no reason not to have them share equally, so that's what I'm going to do—50% to the college fund, 25% to Mike, and 25% to Loretta.

Think about your initial beneficiaries and complete the following:

_____ All initial beneficiaries have equal access to all of the assets (i.e., the assets will be held in a single pot and not divided)

_____ Divide access to the residuary assets among the initial beneficiaries as follows:

Beneficiary	% or $ amount
_____	_____
_____	_____
_____	_____
_____	_____
_____	_____

Now you know what will first happen to your residue when you die—it will be available to the names listed above in the percentages indicated. (We'll determine later how the beneficiaries will be able to use their funds.) If you're not satisfied with your decisions, keep working on them until you are.

Step Five: Subsequent Beneficiaries

For each initial beneficiary, we now need to determine what happens to that beneficiary's share when the beneficiary dies or the share's purpose has been accomplished (e.g., you have funds set aside for college expenses and the beneficiary graduates leaving funds remaining). The remaining funds may go to a new beneficiary or they may be added to funds that are already set aside for another purpose. Examples:

- initial beneficiary is your spouse; when your spouse dies, next beneficiaries are your children

- initial beneficiary is your godchild for college expenses; when your godchild graduates, any remaining funds get added to your spouse's share

- initial beneficiary is your mother; if your mother does not outlive you, her share goes to her church

Go through the "what next" exercise for each beneficiary on your list, starting with your initial "A" beneficiaries and working in the remaining beneficiaries as appropriate. Eventually, your plan should cover as many of your beneficiaries as you decide is realistic and should end in one of the following ways:

- whatever is left goes outright to members of a group that includes so many people that you *know* someone will be alive to receive the remainder (works with large families); or

- whatever is left goes to charity.

Why? Because, as you know, the future is unpredictable. It's not just that you may outlive all of the members of your immediate family; it is also possible (and probably more likely) that a beneficiary will die without having used up all of the funds you set aside for him or her. What then? If you haven't specified what is to happen, you have both lost the opportunity to direct the disposition of your assets and created a loose end that someone will have to fix.

Pat's answer: Hmm. I have two "joint" initial beneficiaries, my spouse Lee and my sister Beth. If Beth dies first, it's easy—Lee becomes the sole beneficiary, and then when Lee dies, the kids get their shares. But if Lee dies first, I don't want Beth to be the sole beneficiary of my entire residue for the rest of her life; a promise is a promise but that's going too far. Anyway, the kids shouldn't have to wait until Beth dies to get their inheritance. If Lee dies first, then I'll set aside 25% for Beth and the other 75% can be divided right away among my three children. I think that's fair, and I think my parents would agree. When Beth dies, whatever is left of her share can be divided among the children, or, if there aren't any, then to grandchildren. With three kids making grandchildren like bunnies, I don't think I have to worry about running out of takers!

Chris's answer: Anything left over from the college fund will go to the community foundation, so my only real question is what happens if Mike or Loretta dies before me. They both have families, but I'm not particularly close to any of their family members so I don't see why I should use them as back-up beneficiaries. Let me go back and look at my checklist... No, I feel like I'm just hunting around for names, and this is too important for that. I know! Mike and I both care about animals; if he dies before me, his share can go to the local no-kill shelter in his memory. And since Loretta and I both went to the same university, I'll name the university to receive her share if she dies before me. That feels good.

Now it's your turn. Fill in your initial beneficiaries and go from there:

Initial beneficiary	Otherwise/then to	Otherwise/then to	Otherwise/then to
_____ →	_____ →	_____ →	_____
_____ →	_____ →	_____ →	_____
_____ →	_____ →	_____ →	_____
_____ →	_____ →	_____ →	_____
_____ →	_____ →	_____ →	_____

Step Six: One Last Review

By now you should have a good idea in your mind of how your residue should flow. Now is the time to plug in your ballpark net worth figure again and see if any final modifications need to be made. Are you leaving enough to your most important beneficiaries, or have you over-diluted their shares through too many specific bequests or the inclusion of too many lesser beneficiaries? If so, you may have to simplify your goals. Conversely, if you are in the wonderful position of having more to give than you think some of your beneficiaries need or deserve, reallocate a portion to other beneficiaries or consider adding some new beneficiaries to the scheme.

Your final plan may be as simple as all to a single charity at your death or it may have several tiers of beneficiaries stretched out over time. Always remember that these are *your* choices—it's *your* legacy—and so the right answer is the one that makes you feel satisfied. Spend as long as it takes to fine-tune your plan until you are happy with it.

Step Seven: Summarize Your Plan

Once you're satisfied with the plan in your head, you need to get it down on paper. Feel free to write it in words, create a chart, draw a picture—whatever way you can communicate it best. (Don't worry; you won't be graded on neatness or creativity.) Ready? Have at it:

Take comfort in the knowledge that what you just accomplished is the most conceptual (and therefore hardest, for many people) part of your decision-making process. It all gets easier from here on out.

Disinheritance

One final thing before we leave the beneficiary identification process behind. Until now, we have been focusing on people you *want* to include in your distribution plan; now it's time to consider people you specifically *don't* want to include. As you know, no one other than your spouse has a legal right to inherit from you. However, if your plan omits someone who normally would be expected to be included—a "natural object of your bounty"—you need to make it clear that the omission was not accidental. In general, "natural object" would include a child, possibly an adopted child or step-child, and possibly an unnamed member of a class of named beneficiaries (e.g., you name "my grandchildren Ann, Bobby, Chris, Debbie, and Elizabeth" but fail to say anything about Fred, whom you intended to omit). If there is anyone who could be a natural object of your bounty whom you want to disinherit, write their names down here and be sure to alert your attorney:

I specifically do not want these people to be beneficiaries of my residue:

_____

_____

_____

When and How Do They Get It?

Now that you know who should get your residue, you need to think about how that residue should be distributed. At its most basic, this decision boils down to how much control you want to—or feel that you need to—maintain after your death.

Types of Control

There are several parameters by which you can control what happens to your assets after you're gone. These include the timing of outright distributions, standards for interim distributions, and "cut off" provisions.

Timing of outright distributions

One way to structure your plan is to provide for outright distributions to a beneficiary—the beneficiary receives a check (or a transfer of funds to the beneficiary's bank account) and the beneficiary is free to do anything at all with the funds from there.

Some people find this concept unsettling, and there certainly are potential downsides to outright distributions. They include:

- The beneficiary may waste the funds. You worked hard to provide for your child, you tried to instill a solid sense of financial responsibility—and your child takes his outright distribution and blows it all in Las Vegas. Or he sinks it all into his dream of opening a restaurant and he's broke six months later. Or he simply lives like a king for a couple of years and before he knows it, the money is gone. It happens.

- The beneficiary may lose motivation. What does the stereotypical "rich kid" do with his life? Not much. He never finds a passion or calling; he never knows the satisfaction of working hard and making his own success. A substantial outright distribution, even if it is not frittered away, can dampen the beneficiary's motivation to, for want of a better description, make something of himself.

- The distribution will be subject to the reach of the beneficiary's spouse and creditors. Once your hard-earned funds are in your beneficiary's pocket, they can be seized by anyone to whom the beneficiary owes a legal obligation. This can include garden variety creditors, but it also can include someone who sues your beneficiary and obtains a judgment—maybe your beneficiary is in a car accident and the other driver is awarded an amount greater than your beneficiary's insurance limits. It can also include a soon-to-be-ex-spouse who wants a piece of your beneficiary's wealth. Funds retained in a properly-drafted trust, on the other hand, can be protected from this type of loss.

- The distribution may impact the beneficiary's ability to qualify for assistance. If your beneficiary develops a disability and wishes to apply for government assistance programs, assets held in his own name (including the outright distribution from your residue) can result in disqualification until the assets are "spent down." Similarly, if your beneficiary is in college, most need-based grants and scholarships will disappear if he suddenly has a substantial nest egg in his own name.

Do these downsides cause you concern with respect to one (or some, or all) of your beneficiaries? Jot down what you're thinking:

Beneficiary	Reason for concern

With all of those downsides, why would anyone ever provide for an outright distribution? There are upsides as well, including:

- Cost savings and convenience. Keeping funds out of a beneficiary's hands requires a trust, and trusts don't run themselves. Even if the trustee you have chosen refuses to accept a fee, the trust will still run up accounting fees, investment fees, account maintenance fees, and so forth. Once the value of the trust drops below a certain amount, it frankly becomes uneconomical to maintain. Do you really want to pay to keep a trust alive if each beneficiary's share wouldn't even pay for a decent vacation?

- Encourage independence. Having a trustee guarding the castle gates may protect your beneficiary, but it also can inhibit independence. While some beneficiaries may lose motivation if they receive an outright distribution that leaves them set for life (or at least for a long time), others lose motivation to grow up and become independent if they know that a check for their living expenses will arrive on the first of the month forever. This type of beneficiary will feel—and act—like an adult much more quickly if given complete control over his or her life. How do you know with certainty which type of beneficiary you have? You don't. No one said estate planning was easy.

- Vote of confidence. Even if your beneficiary is well versed in the wisdom of trust arrangements, on some level he still may feel that you tied up his inheritance because you didn't trust him to manage it wisely. Providing for an outright distribution—or a number of outright distributions over time—may help alleviate those feelings.

If you're concerned about the downsides of outright distributions but don't want to lose the benefit of the upsides, you can take a middle ground: Provide for partial outright distributions at various points in time. Typical distribution schemes include:

- outright distributions of set dollar amounts when the beneficiary reaches certain milestones—graduates from college, gets married, has a child, etc.

- partial outright distributions of a percentage of the trust assets as the beneficiary reaches certain ages (typically something like 25, 30, and 35)

- partial outright distributions of a percentage of the trust assets based on how long the beneficiary has been a beneficiary (for example, one-third of the assets five years after the beneficiary's trust comes into existence)

- outright distribution of the balance if the trust balance falls below a certain value

Scheduled partial distributions are less risky than complete outright distributions, but they still raise the possibility that the distribution will be lost to creditors, predators, or the beneficiary's poor judgment. Unless you know that a beneficiary's share will be small, leaving distribution discretion with the trustee often is the best way to go.

Interim Distribution Standards

The trustee almost always is given the authority to use funds for the beneficiary's benefit as long as the trust is in existence. As the person creating the trust, you get to define what that authority looks like. (Note that in certain cases the standards you choose can have significant tax consequences; listen to your attorney if you're told you "have" to include certain provisions.)

In most cases, it is best to give the trustee broad discretion and leave it at that. There simply is no way to predict what the future will hold; specific instructions may lead to consequences far different than you would have wished. However, there are many flavors of discretion. Consider the following general descriptions:

- Minimal support. The trustee's authority can be limited to providing for a beneficiary's basic needs only. "Basic needs" might be as minimal as shelter, food, and medical care. If you have a limited pool of funds and want to make it work as a safety net for several people, this might be a good option.

- "Basic plus." You can provide authority for the trust to pay for a beneficiary's basic needs plus certain additional activities that are important to you, such as higher education, travel, or philanthropic opportunities.

- Health, Education, Maintenance, and Support. This is probably the most commonly used standard, and it covers more or less everything you would expect a trust to cover. Heart transplant? Covered. Annual around-the-world odysseys? Not covered. College expenses? Covered. Monthly payments to loan shark? Not covered.

- Best interests. "Best interests" is a broad standard that can include distributions to start or expand a business, relocate to a more favorable environment, pursue a career change, delve into a satisfying hobby, and so forth. Essentially, the trustee can distribute funds for any purpose which, on balance, is good for the beneficiary.

- Complete discretion. You can give the trustee the authority to distribute funds to the beneficiary for any purpose the trustee deems acceptable. This is an extremely broad standard (almost not a standard at all) and may impact the tax and asset protection benefits of having a trust in the first place. Your attorney can provide guidance on this issue.

The type of standard you choose is a function of what you want to accomplish. Remember that this is your decision and no one else's.

"Cut off" provisions

Technically, it is possible to terminate a beneficiary's interest in the trust upon the occurrence of a certain event—a classic example is the "Junior gets the trust fund provided he is married by his thirtieth birthday" movie plot. This provision may make for a good movie, but it makes for a terrible estate plan. No matter how strongly you may feel about the goodness or badness of certain behavior, completely terminating someone's interest—someone who is important enough to you to be a trust beneficiary in the first place—is an incredibly drastic step that simply should not be set in stone. Let your trustee know your feelings and leave it to him or her to make the right decisions down the line.

Now it's time to pull everything together. For each of your beneficiaries, you need to decide when (if ever) funds should be subject to mandatory outright distribution and what the funds can be used for in the meantime. The following sections will discuss a number of common beneficiary types and the decisions they require; if a particular section doesn't apply to you, feel free to skip it and move on.

Provisions for Spouses

If you are married, it's likely that your spouse is your number one beneficiary and will be the primary focus of your distribution plan during his or her lifetime. If your estate plan is or may become large enough to warrant tax planning (ask your attorney), there are specific provisions that will need to be included in order to accomplish your tax-avoidance goals, and you need to follow your attorney's advice with respect to those provisions. However, there are some general non-legal decisions that need to come from you. They include:

Outright distributions v. retention in trust. If your net worth is relatively modest, your spouse is financially savvy (or at least financially stable), and your assets are likely to be used up relatively quickly, you might be best served to take the simple path and just leave everything to your spouse outright. However, if any of the following are true in your situation, a trust arrangement might be a better option:

____ Your spouse has no idea how to manage money.

____ You want to make sure that there is something left for your #2 (and perhaps subsequent) beneficiaries.

____ Your spouse may be susceptible to smooth-talking scam artists.

____ Your spouse is engaged in a profession which raises asset protection concerns.

The pros and cons of each approach can be summarized thusly:

Approach	Pros	Cons
Outright Distribution	- Simple - Cost-effective	- No tax planning possible - No asset protection - Spouse can leave your assets to anyone; no guarantee that your #2 beneficiaries will receive anything
Retention in Trust	- Protects spouse from poor decisions and predators - Facilitates tax planning - More likely that your #2 beneficiaries will benefit - Spouse's future creditors cannot reach assets	- Ongoing trust expense - May limit spouse's ability to alter distribution plan in light of future events

Consider the pros and cons as they apply to your own situation and decide which alternative you prefer:

_____ Distribute outright to my spouse

- or -

_____ Retain assets in trust for my spouse

Level of support. In a typical family situation (spouse plus children), assuming assets remain in trust, you need to think about what level of support your spouse should enjoy and how that decision ultimately impacts what your children will receive. After all, the more your spouse consumes, the less your kids will receive in the end.

See if one of these strikes a chord with you; if so, check it off:

_____ My sole concern is my spouse's well-being. The trust assets should be used to make my spouse happy and comfortable even if it means that nothing is left for my children at my spouse's death.

_____ I want my spouse's needs to be balanced against my children's eventual inheritance; while my spouse should not be deprived of a comfortable level of support, I would be disappointed if my children received no inheritance.

_____ I expect my spouse to provide for him/herself after my death. My trust assets should only be used as a safety net for my spouse; my primary goal is to leave as much as possible to my children.

Of course, the same trade-off exists even if you have no children; your #2 beneficiary will receive more or less depending upon how much is spent to support your spouse. The only real differences are that many people feel a particular obligation to leave money to their children, and often—especially when children are young—funds spent on the spouse benefit the children as well.

If your #2 beneficiary is someone other than your children, it may be easier to consider your spouse's level of support without regard to other beneficiaries. Try this—make a mark on the following scale to indicate your intentions:

Pay only for basic needs
that my spouse can't cover
on his or her own

Pay for the standard of
living we have now

Spare no expense

Your attorney may or may not use this information while drafting your documents, but it will be valuable to your trustee in any case.

Other guidance. Most of the following decisions won't (and probably shouldn't) end up as an official part of your estate plan, but they will help you clarify your thoughts and focus the picture of what you want the world to be like after you're gone. You should share these thoughts with your spouse as well as your trustee.

- Do you expect your spouse to work? Let's say you want your spouse to be supported at the same standard of living you both were enjoying at the time of your death. Should your spouse have to contribute to that standard? If you have minor children, you may want your spouse to be able to remain (or become) a full-time parent, but consider the effect that would have on the trust's ability to support your spouse long-term and still have something left for your children in the future. While you may not want to *require* your spouse to work (what if he or she can't find a job or becomes disabled?), you should let your spouse and trustee know your philosophy:

____ I want the trust to be the sole source of my spouse's support.

____ I would prefer that my spouse not work while our children are still minors, but I expect my spouse to work thereafter.

____ I expect my spouse to make a good faith effort to contribute to his or her own support.

____ The trust should only pay what's necessary for my spouse's basic support; anything additional should come from his or her own efforts.

- Remarriage. If your spouse remarries, should his or her new spouse's resources be taken into consideration?

____ The new spouse's resources should not be considered.

____ The new spouse's resources should be considered but the trust should still be considered a primary source of support.

____ To the extent possible, if my spouse remarries, the trust assets should be preserved for my children or other subsequent beneficiaries and not used for my spouse's support.

Provisions for Children

Many people find this to be one of the most difficult parts of planning. You know your spouse; he or she is an adult and unlikely to change appreciably over time. If you leave your assets to charity, you know the charity's purpose and how your assets will be used. But kids? Who can predict? No one, that's who.

Before you start making decisions, there are a couple of concepts that deserve careful consideration.

Multiple children – when to divide the pot. In a typical plan, the trust benefits the spouse during his or her lifetime and then splits into separate shares for the children upon the spouse's death. It is possible, however, to keep the trust in a single pot for all of the children until the youngest child reaches a specified age. Why would you do that?

- If the trust is divided into shares when the children are young and one child goes through a crisis (say a medical struggle) during childhood, his or her share will bear the entire financial burden—perhaps leaving nothing left for that child when he or she reaches adulthood. On the other hand, if you had still been alive, the crisis would have been met using family funds, and the affected child would not have been penalized. Which outcome is fair?

- If separate shares are created when the children are still young, the youngest child's share will be depleted at a proportionately higher level just to get the child to adulthood. In other words, while you may have intended that each child inherit the same amount (that's why you divided the trust into equal shares in the first place), the younger child will actually have less when he or she reaches the age of majority because more will be spent on from his or her share on his or her support during childhood.

Maintaining a single pot until all of the children are grown is not without downsides, however. These downsides include:

- The eldest child may deplete the pot for higher education (Harvard, anyone?) before the younger children have a chance to receive their "equal" share.

- If there is a fairly wide age gap, maintaining a single pot may force the older child to wait well into adulthood before his or her share is established and available for distribution. For example, say you have two children ages 15 and 13 and a third child (perhaps from a second marriage) who is age 2. If you wait until the youngest child is age 18 before dividing the trust into shares, the eldest child will be 31 before his or her individual share is established.

What is the right answer for you? Only you can say. Generally, if your children are young and close in age, the pros of waiting until the children are adults to divide the trust into separate shares probably outweigh the cons. If your children are already adults or if there is a large age discrepancy, an immediate division may make more sense.

My Plan: _____ immediate division _____ delayed division

Make decisions child-by-child. Most parents want to be fair to their children, and most interpret that to mean that each child gets an equal share distributed in the same way. As a parent myself, I understand this reasoning: If everything is equal, no one can feel slighted and no one can read anything negative into my actions. It's the easy way out.

But we're talking about something a bit more important here than who gets the biggest cookie. You need to think carefully about each child individually and do what's right for *that* child, not force all of your children into the same mold and hope for the best.

True story: The first time I administered an estate with different distribution provisions (outright to Child A; in trust for life for Child B), I thought the world was going to end. Child B was furious. He railed against his heartless mother; he told me how she had always favored his sister and had never given him his due. I really felt bad for this guy—until I got to know more about him. He hadn't held a steady job in years. He had drug issues. He had legal issues. There was no reason to keep Child A's portion in trust—she was stable and responsible—but if Child B had received his inheritance outright, it would have been gone in no time.

Your child doesn't need to be a drug addict to warrant special treatment, and outright-or-trust isn't the only way to differentiate among your children. Consider these possibilities:

1) Unequal division. Are your children identical? They why should their inheritances be identical? If your children are older and one is already financially set, at least consider limiting that child's involvement in your financial estate. Talk to the child about it—you may find that he or she would rather see your money go to less-well-off siblings.

Do you think you should consider unequal division? ____ Yes ____ No ____ Maybe

2) Different distribution pattern. If you choose to provide for distributions at certain ages, don't assume that the ages should be the same for each child. When your children are young, there may be nothing upon which to base different treatment—personalities and life plans take time to develop—but as the children grow, you will see more and more hints of what their futures may look like. Consider those hints. If they lead you to make a different decision for one child than for another, then that is what you should do.

Let's say that as a general rule, you think a child beneficiary should receive a distribution of one-third of the trust at age 25, one-third at age 30, and the balance at age 35. This is a pretty standard distribution pattern and it works just fine in many cases. You think it would work just fine for two of your three children, but you're unsure of the third. Why might you be unsure?

- The child is pursuing (or already engaged in) a risky career. If your child is in a profession that carries a risk of being sued—medicine, law, architecture, construction, the list grows daily—then both you and the child may prefer that the trust remain in place indefinitely so that the assets will be protected from future judgments.

- The child is taking a while to "find himself." Some people take longer to grow up than others, and there's nothing wrong with that. If you have a late bloomer in your family, you might want to adjust your distribution plan for that child accordingly—perhaps set distributions at ages 35, 40, and 45 rather than the 25, 30, and 35 you plan for your other children.

- The child has drug, gambling, or judgment issues. You know that giving this child a substantial outright distribution would be a mistake (if not a disaster), but you don't want to tie up your other children's funds unnecessarily. The only responsible choice is to specify a different distribution pattern for the troubled child.

- The child doesn't need any outright distributions. Perhaps this child has already become established financially and a distribution from your trust would be unnecessary. Again, maintaining a single distribution pattern for this child and his or her siblings would not be in everyone's best interests.

There are many other situations which would suggest different distribution patterns for different children, but I bet you already get the point: You should think about each child individually and make the best choices you can for that child.

Consider each child in turn and decide when (if ever) the child should receive scheduled outright distributions. Remember that the funds will always be available for the child; what we're talking about now are mandatory outright distributions built into the trust document.

Child	Distribution pattern
_____	_____
_____	_____
_____	_____

3) Different support standards. Just as different distribution patterns may make sense, so may different standards governing the level of support a child receives from the trust. The difference here is that in most cases, leaving broad discretion to the trustee will accomplish what you want—a trustee charged with distributing funds in a child's best interests, for example, would not make a large distribution to an addict or to a child who had no need or desire for the distribution. Therefore the only real reasons to adopt different support standards are to:

- Control behavior. Let's say (just between us) that one of your children is terminally lazy. We're talking no motivation whatsoever. You believe in your heart that if this child can live comfortably—not even extravagantly and not even forever—off of the trust fund, then the child will do nothing else. You don't want your assets to contribute to this child's lack of initiative, but you don't want to restrict your other children's support unnecessarily. What do you do? Perhaps you limit the unmotivated child to basic support, at least for a period of time.

- Make a point. Sometimes parents and children have irreconcilable differences—political, religious, lifestyle, whatever—that can't be set aside. Some parents simply leave that child out of their estate plan, but for other parents, taking that step is unthinkable. At the same time, they cannot in good conscience pretend that the differences don't exist, and they do not want their assets seen to be supporting something they cannot abide. One option is to leave funds in trust for the child as a safety net, but limit distributions to a very minimal support standard.

Do you need to consider different support standards? ___ Yes ___ No ___ Maybe

Provisions for Charities

Leaving money to charity is about as easy as it gets. There are just a couple of points to consider.

- Name the right charity. By "name the right charity," I don't mean name a good charity or a charity that I like or anything like that; I mean name the charity you intend to name. Many charities have similar names, and many charities have local chapters that are legally distinct from the parent organization. Some organizations are supported by multiple foundations, each with a different purpose and focus. If you don't get the legal name exactly right, you risk confusion at best and a court action at worst.

The best way to ensure that your money goes where it should go is to contact your intended charity (or visit its website) and confirm its legal name. If you have charities on your beneficiary list, take the time now to research their legal names:

Charity	Legal name confirmed

- General fund v. specific purpose. If you don't specify otherwise, your donation will be added to the charity's general fund and used wherever it is needed most. If you have something more specific in mind—perhaps you want your gift to go to your university's scholarship fund rather than its general fund—you need to say so. If you have specifics in mind, note them here:

Charity	Specific Purpose

- Alternatives to outright bequests. If charity is a significant focus of your distribution intentions, you should investigate more sophisticated planning techniques such as charitable lead or remainder trusts, pooled funds, or private foundations. These are well outside the scope of this book and should be explored with an attorney.

Trusts for Education

One goal of many people is to provide for the education of their loved ones—children, grandchildren, nieces and nephews, and so on. In some cases, these beneficiaries already have a trust carved out for their general benefit and education will be paid from there. In other cases, a dollar amount or percentage is set aside specifically for the education of a class of beneficiaries. If this is part of your plan, you need to consider the issues that follow.

Defining the beneficiary class. Let's say you want to designate $200,000 to be used for your grandchildren's college expenses, and you have four grandchildren right now. Are you likely to have additional grandchildren before you die? If so, do you mean to include them? If a grandchild is born after your death, should he or she have access to the trust benefits? There are no right or wrong answers; what you intend is what should happen. Give it some thought and then select your choice:

_____ The beneficiary class should be limited to those who are living when I execute my estate plan.

_____ The beneficiary class should be limited to those who are living when I die.

___ The class should be limited to those living at a point I specify, such as five years after my death. That point is _____.

_____ The class should remain open as long as possible.

When (and if) to divide into shares. This is the same issue we discussed in the Provisions for Children section, but it takes on a slightly different flavor if the purpose of the fund is limited to education and the funds are available to a potentially expanding class. First, unlike medical or other support needs, the choice of which college to attend is just that—a choice—and an individual beneficiary will not be irreparably harmed if there are not enough funds in his or her share to pay for a top-notch college. Second, if you are going to leave the class open for a period of time after your death, then as a logical matter dividing the trust into shares at the time of your death is impossible.

If you want to ensure that everyone in the class receives equal treatment, then you need to close the class at or before the time of your death (i.e., no one born later gets any benefit) and split the gross allocation into shares immediately when you die. But what happens if one beneficiary needs more than his or her share while another needs less? Should one share be able to "borrow" from another, perhaps by accessing the unused balance of an already-graduated beneficiary? On the other hand, if you don't divide the trust into shares but instead leave it as a single pot, then each beneficiary has an equal right to the entire fund. Doesn't that encourage each beneficiary to attend the most expensive (not necessarily best) college possible, so as to obtain maximum benefit from your trust? Is that what you want?

There is no perfect solution here. If you are fortunate enough to be able to devote a large amount to education for a small class of beneficiaries, then a single pot approach should work just fine. If you have more limited funds and you want to make sure that younger beneficiaries are covered, then you may want to divide the funds into individual shares instead.

To cap or not to cap?. One way to keep the funds in a single pot but ensure that everyone gets something is to cap each beneficiary's distribution at a specific dollar amount. For example, if you designate $200,000 for your grandchildren's education and place a cap of $20,000 on each beneficiary, you will know that you have covered at least ten grandchildren—perhaps more, if some of the first ten do not use their entire allotment.

Termination and distribution. At some point—when all beneficiaries have graduated from college, when the youngest beneficiary reaches a specified age, or otherwise as you decide—the education trust will terminate. If it is still holding funds, where should those funds go? Here are some ideas:

- Add the funds to another trust. If there is an existing trust for your spouse, children, or other beneficiaries, you can direct that the education trust funds be transferred to the other existing trust(s). (Note: There may be tax reasons not to add the funds to a trust for your spouse, depending upon that trust's terms and purpose.)

- Distribute to the education trust's beneficiaries. If you intended the trust to benefit those people, then it may make sense to you to give them the left-overs.

- Distribute to an educational institution. The existence of the trust indicates that you value education; you may wish to further prove your commitment by donating any remaining funds to an educational institution, either to its general fund or to its scholarship fund.

These are only suggestions; you can do anything you want with the remaining funds.

If you are planning an education trust, complete the following:

Amount or percentage to allocate: _____

Beneficiaries: _____

Class includes those living at

_____ the execution of my estate plan

_____ my death

_____ _____ years after my death

_____ at any time before the trust terminates

When trust is to terminate: _____

Distribution of any remainder at the end of the trust goes to: _____

Summarizing Your Plan

You now know who should participate in your estate plan and what their participation should look like. Take a moment now to complete the Estate Plan Blueprint in the Appendix so that all of your decisions are in one place. Once you're finished, you will be ready to move on to Part Four and make your plan a reality.

PART FOUR:
MAKING THE PLAN A REALITY

If you've made it this far, then the hard part is done—all that's left is to pull your decisions together into a coherent whole, get your documents drafted, and execute them.

Do You Need a Lawyer?

This guide has been written as if you will work with an attorney to complete your estate plan. But is that really necessary? In the past, the answer to this question would have been an immediate yes; lawyers knew the law and nobody else had a clue. More to the point, nobody else *wanted* to have a clue. Simply put, there were areas of life—law and medicine, to name two—that the average person was content to leave to the professionals.

Not so today, of course. We like to feel self-directed and in control, as the explosion of self-helps books and online resources can attest. We google our symptoms and *then* go to the doctor, and if the doctor's diagnosis doesn't agree with our own, we're suspicious. Does the doctor know what he's doing? Is he just ordering tests for the sake of lining his pockets? What makes him so smart, anyway?

It's the same thing with law, and relevant to this conversation, estate planning. Somewhere along the way someone realized that Wills and trusts were just documents, words on paper, and it didn't take a mystic to get the right words onto the paper. As self-help resources became more sophisticated and easily accessible, many people decided to do the job themselves. And that's okay—sometimes. But sometimes it's not, and it can be difficult to decide which camp you fall into.

Factors to Consider

So do you need a lawyer or not? I can't tell you, but I can give you some things to think about. I would strongly suggest contacting an attorney if any of these situations apply to you:

- Your gross estate (everything you own) is worth a significant amount. What constitutes "significant?" For estate tax purposes, that amount has changed over time and currently is more or less impossible to predict. To be on the safe side, I would talk to an attorney for any gross estate (note: that's gross estate, not the net worth figure we have been referencing) over $1 million, even if you have no complications that would raise legal issues.

- You own a business. You need to think about what should happen to the business after you're gone—the sale of your interest to partners or to an outside entity, transfer to your spouse or children, etc.—and a lawyer is well-suited to work you through those issues.

- You have special family circumstances. No family is "normal" (at least none that I've ever seen), but some are more functional than others. If you have a blended family from multiple marriages, a disabled child, contentious relationships, or responsibility (legal or moral) for a non-family member, you should talk to a lawyer.

- You are in a same-sex relationship. There are some very good self-help resources out there for same-sex couples, but given the changing and therefore hopelessly confused state of current law, I still would recommend working with a lawyer.

Even if you don't necessarily need a lawyer, you may want one. Lawyers are good for more than dotting Is and crossing Ts. Some additional benefits to consider:

- Your estate plan will get done. Face it, if you leave it to your own motivation, you may never finish your documents. Engaging a lawyer brings someone else into the picture, and that someone else will hold you accountable for doing your part in moving the process along. For some people, this is the only way to ensure that the plan is completed.

- Apparent authority. A Will prepared by an attorney carries more weight than one prepared by a layman—not necessarily legally, but in the eyes of the public. If you have any inkling at all that someone may challenge your intentions, it's a good idea to have an attorney behind your documents from the very beginning.

- Someone to turn to. When you die, your family members will have enough to tackle without worrying about financial details and legal procedures. If you have an attorney who is familiar with you and your estate plan, one call from the family can set the legal procedures in motion.

Finally, before deciding to draft your own documents, consider this:

Do you really want to go the cheap route?

There are only two reasons I can think of to complete your estate plan yourself: No lawyers are available in your geographical location (ha) or you don't want to pay a lawyer to draft your documents. Assuming it's the latter, consider whether this is a good place to cut corners—these documents will control who makes decisions that directly impact you and everyone you care about, and ultimately will control what happens to everything you own. I'm a big fan of independent spirit, but is this the best place to flex your do-it-yourself muscles?

A basic estate plan will cost a few hundred dollars; a more comprehensive one will cost a little more. For this, you get access to a professional who will answer your questions, explain legal planning techniques that may save your beneficiaries money, and produce documents that (presumably) will do what you want and do it to the letter of the law. Sounds like a bargain to me.

Choosing a Lawyer

If you decide to work with a lawyer, you will need to select one. Here are some pointers on how to go about finding a good one for your needs:

Ask around. Personal recommendations work for auto mechanics, they work for plumbers, and they also work for attorneys. Ask your local friends if they have worked with a lawyer recently (tell them you're working on your estate plan so they don't think you're getting divorced or going to jail), and if so, what they thought of their experience. If you keep hearing the same name in a positive light (or, in a smaller town, if you hear any name in a positive light), put that name on your list of possibilities.

Stop reading for a second, pick up the phone, and call (text, email, whatever) a few of your friends. Also look for recommendations from professionals with whom you're already working; your accountant or financial advisor may have strong opinions based on past experience—good or bad—with local estate planners. (Keep in mind, of course, that those opinions may be colored by professional referral arrangements.)

Make a list of possibilities based on what you hear:

Potential lawyers:

1) _____

2) _____

3) _____

4) _____

5) _____

Specialization. Most lawyers specialize to some extent, but most do not limit themselves to one area of practice. In general, the larger the community the more likely you will be to find specialists; for obvious and logical reasons, smaller-town lawyers tend to be generalists. Do you need a specialist? It depends on your situation, of course. As a general rule:

- If you have a very small estate and all you really need are documents that leave everything to a single person and (if applicable) name a guardian for your kids, then any competent general practice lawyer should be able to meet your needs.

- If you have more significant assets and/or you want to place limits on when distributions can be made (signs that you may benefit from a trust arrangement), you should be looking for an attorney who focuses on estate planning as a major practice area, although he or she is likely to do other legal work as well.

- If you have a very large estate, need sophisticated tax planning, and/or want to establish charitable or multigenerational trusts, you need to find a true specialist whose primary (if not sole) practice area is estate planning.

How do you know if one of your prospective lawyers is a specialist? Many communities have local estate planning councils; if a lawyer is a member of one of these, you can probably assume that he or she has a focus on estate planning. You can look in your yellow pages to see if the lawyer has chosen to be listed under Estate Planning, but don't take that indication as gospel—some very good estate planners don't bother to pay the extra charge for specialty listings, while some all-purpose lawyers list themselves under every practice area available. The best approach may be to simply call the lawyer's office and ask what type of work the lawyer does. If the answer is "oh, just about anything," you have a generalist (again, not a bad thing unless you need more).

Go back to your list and cross off anyone who does not seem to be a good fit with your needs.

Responsiveness. You may not want someone who is obviously desperate for clients, but you do want someone who will call you back within a reasonable time and who can see you sooner than six months from Monday. Responsiveness is important if only because it's a sign of professionalism. Call the names on your list and leave a message asking for a return call. Individual tolerance levels may vary, but if I were you, I would cross off anyone who doesn't call you back within 48 hours.

Personal impression. You want to be comfortable with your estate planner, and you want to enjoy working with him or her. If you talk to a prospective match over the phone and you simply don't like what you hear, move on. There are plenty of other fish in the sea.

Cost. While cost shouldn't be the only factor in selecting your estate planning lawyer, sometimes fees can tell you something about the lawyer's practice. Someone who quotes a fee significantly higher than you hear from other lawyers probably has a very specialized practice and is used to working with very wealthy people who need sophisticated planning. If that's not you, then the higher cost may not be worth it. On the other hand, a quote significantly lower than other lawyers probably means that the lawyer a) rarely does estate planning and is completely out of touch with current average fees (not good for you), or

b) is so desperate for clients that he or she will undercut the norm just to earn anything possible (not good for you unless the lawyer is new to your area and is trying to build a practice).

How do you get a cost estimate? Sometimes it's not as simple as asking; some lawyers base their fees strictly on the time it actually takes to accomplish the task and adamantly refuse to quote anything but the broadest ballpark estimate at the outset. As a lawyer, I understand their position. Most lawyers have at one time or another quoted a fee up front only to discover that the facts are complicated or the client is difficult and the work is going to take much longer than usual—and you can bet that the client will not happily accept a final fee larger than the initial quote. The lawyer often has to write off the additional time, and that is both frustrating and unfair.

However, the majority of estate plans are fairly predictable in terms of the effort they will require, so any experienced estate planner should be able to give you a decent ballpark estimate. Many charge flat fees for their work with the fees tied to the documents produced. In either case, you should feel comfortable with the flat or estimated fee before you proceed.

Go back to your original list and do the following:

- Cross off anyone who doesn't fit your needs from a specialization standpoint.

- Cross off anyone who didn't respond to your initial phone call in what you consider to be a timely manner.

- Cross off anyone whose fees are unreasonable or beyond your ability to pay.

- Cross off anyone you simply don't like.

If you have no names left on your list, don't despair; just go back to asking your friends, colleagues, and professional advisors for recommendations. If need be, you can do an online search or simply refer to the yellow pages, although obviously a recommendation from someone you know can be more enlightening.

Going It Alone

If you consider all of the above and decide that you want to do your own estate planning documents, there are resources both in print and online to which you can turn. Any such resource should provide you with forms *specific to your state of residence* and should provide you with clear instructions on how to execute the documents, including which ones need to be witnessed and which ones need to be notarized. If you are using an online estate planning tool, typically you will fill out an online questionnaire that will then be used to generate your documents. If the decisions you have made don't appear as an option on the questionnaire, *don't change your decisions to fit the tool*; find another tool. If the resource you are using suggests that you need to talk to an attorney (the Nolo Press series is particularly good about this), then for heaven's sake talk to an attorney. Regardless of the resource you select, do *not* alter the documents unless—and if you do, only to the extent that—the resource says you can.

Working With Your Lawyer (If You Use One)

When you meet with your attorney, don't be surprised if he or she is surprised that you know what you want—remember, most people really don't. Lay out your decisions and then listen to what the attorney has to say. He or she may have suggestions or insights that you had not considered; if so, don't hesitate to change your mind. After all, the attorney is a professional with training and experience, not just a scrivener.

True story: I received a call from a man who wanted me to draft a Will for him. Actually what he said was "I know exactly what I want; I just need for you to type it up." Good thing I took that typing class in high school, huh?

While you should listen to your attorney's thoughts, don't automatically trash your plan and do whatever he or she says. With all due respect to my legal brethren (and I mean that), there may be factors at play that have nothing to do with the legitimacy of your intentions. These include:

- Your plan doesn't fit the attorney's forms. We talked earlier about how fond estate planners are of their form books. If what you want is at all unusual, the attorney's unconscious response may be "how on earth am I going to draft *that* provision?!?" To avoid being bothered with extra work, the attorney may (again, unconsciously) try to talk you into an easier plan.

- Your plan isn't traditional. Remember that estate planners tend to be conservative when it comes to their work; if they haven't seen it before, they don't trust it. Don't be surprised if the attorney tries to steer you toward something more mainstream. It's up to you how to respond.

That said, you *should* listen carefully if the attorney wants to modify your plan for legal reasons, especially reasons based on tax implications or state law. Remember your respective roles: You decide what you want and your attorney makes it happen. If it can't happen (or if there are unacceptable consequences in making it happen), you will need to adjust. Working together, you and your attorney should be able to arrive at a final plan that leaves both of you comfortable.

"Bulletproof" Your Plan

Will contests are uncommon, but when they happen, they are a nightmare. In general, the grounds for a Will contest (or a legal dispute that falls short of a formal contest but still causes headaches) fall under one or more of the following categories:

- Incompetence. In this case, someone is going to allege that at the time the Will was executed, you were not legally competent to do so. This is most often seen when someone was elderly and changed the provisions of his or her Will shortly before death, especially if the new Will's provisions varied significantly from prior provisions. As noted above, the standard for competence in connection with executing a Will are actually quite low—the signer only needs to know what he owns, know the "natural objects of his bounty" (the people who normally would expect to inherit), and have intent to do what the document says—but defending against a claim of incompetence can be expensive, time-consuming, and emotionally difficult for the decedent's survivors.

- Undue influence. Undue influence means that someone (usually the one who's receiving something under the Will that someone else thinks he shouldn't) held an excessive degree of physical or mental control over you and used that control to convince you to do something you otherwise would not have done. Essentially, the claim is one of practical incompetence—you were so influenced by the evildoer that you were not able to think clearly.

- Fraud. A fraud claim usually asserts that you made decisions based on promises that the person taking under the Will never intended to keep. For example, a caregiver might have promised to stay with you for the rest of your life if you updated your Will to include him, but then left as soon as you became incompetent.

- Mistake. One example of mistake would be the omission of a child that the testator mistakenly believed to be dead.

- Ambiguity. This category is the most common and the most preventable of all; it happens when the Will is written such that two (or more) reasonable interpretations exist. Unfortunately, if the assets at issue are valuable enough—either in monetary terms or in psychological terms—the issue is likely to end up before a judge.

Ambiguity is likely to arise from one of three areas. The first is drafting error—the document simply is drafted so poorly that it is unclear what the decedent meant to say. Drafting errors can include conflicting provisions (one section dictates one result, another section dictates another result, and it's impossible for both to occur), missing provisions (the Will doesn't indicate what happens to the residuary estate, a more common error than you might think), or long chains of legalistic phrases that simply cannot be parsed into a comprehensible sentence. The potential for drafting error is a great argument in favor of hiring a competent lawyer to draft your documents.

The second likely area of ambiguity is an insufficient description of the property at issue. For example, the Will may state "I leave my blue automobile to Lisa and all of my other automobiles to Ron." What if there are two blue automobiles? What if one of the automobiles was blue when the Will was executed but later was repainted green? How difficult would it have been to describe that automobile as "my 1956 Chevy?"

The third likely area of ambiguity is an insufficient description of the recipient. As discussed above, this often occurs in connection with gifts to charities, where the addition or omission of a word or two can make all the difference. You may know what you meant when you said "to the Heart Association," but you may not know that there are literally scores of individual charities with the words "heart" and "association" in their legal names. If the gift is small, your executor is likely to assume the most logical interpretation and act on that assumption, and no one is likely to object. However, if the gift is large, several charities may have a legitimate claim to the gift, and your executor will have a court battle on his hands.

Ways to Avoid a Will Contest

You can't guarantee that no one will contest your estate plan, but there are actions you can take to minimize the likelihood of a dispute and to minimize the impact of a dispute should one be raised. This can be tricky business, though, so if you have real concerns about someone contesting your Will after your death, be sure to raise them with an attorney. Here are some ideas you and your attorney might want to consider:

- Remove ambiguity. This is a simple one, and you really should do it whether you anticipate a contest or not. Go through your documents and try to identify any potentially ambiguous sections, then fix them. If you are working with an attorney, this should be the attorney's job, but an extra pair of eyes is never a bad thing.

- Communicate the reasons behind your decisions. If you have made decisions that may make someone unhappy, leave a letter explaining your thoughts. This letter has a dual purpose—it helps the disappointed beneficiary understand, and it also gives a probate judge (if it comes to that) a basis for understanding your decision and finding it to be reasonable and legitimate.

- Keep evidence supporting your decisions. The most common challenge to an estate plan comes from a child who does not get what he thinks he should get. The most common reason that the child got what he got is because he neglected his relationship with his parent in the parent's later years. It's pretty simple: "You don't call, you don't write" translates into "You don't get my stuff when I die."

That parent has a right to do as he pleases, but you can guess what's going to happen. The child who took care of the parent and thus ultimately got more than his "fair" share of the estate is going to be accused of exercising undue influence, and the parent won't be around to dispute the claim. The siblings will claim that they tried to stay in touch with Mom or Dad but the controlling caregiver sibling wouldn't let them. The awful horrible caregiver child did everything he or she could do to minimize contact; it was all part of a plot to turn Mom or Dad against the other children so the evil nasty caregiver child could walk away with all the goods.

If this sounds like it could happen to you, think about keeping a diary of your contacts with your children. A calendar full of "called Bobby—no response" entries will help defuse Bobby's argument that he was trying to be a part of your life.

- Act as independently as possible. If you select an attorney independently, get yourself to the attorney's office independently, and talk to the attorney with no one else present, an undue influence claim will be much more difficult to pursue.

- Videotape the execution of your documents. The idea behind videotaping is to provide evidence that you were competent and thinking clearly and independently when you signed your plan documents. This step is unusual (although not unheard of) and should be discussed thoroughly with your attorney.

- Have a mental evaluation. This is a drastic step that could backfire, but if you are very concerned about a challenge based upon your mental state and you want an independent professional opinion to back you up, it is an option. The evaluation should be done by someone with appropriate credentials (obviously) and should occur fairly contemporaneously with the execution of the documents.

Again, if you have serious concerns about someone trying to overturn your estate plan after your death, discuss your concerns with an attorney. You and your attorney can determine whether anything special should be done in connection with the document execution.

Executing Your Documents

Once you have actual printed documents in your hands—whether prepared by an attorney or via a self-help medium—here's what you should do:

1) Read through each document carefully, no matter how painful and boring it may be. Make a note of anything you don't understand or you think may not be consistent with

your plan. Clarify each of these items with your attorney (or do further research if you created the documents yourself) before you sign anything. Repeat: Read and understand your documents before you sign them.

2) Pay attention while signing. Make sure you are signing your own documents (mix-ups are rare but not impossible), that nothing happened when signature copies were being prepared (i.e., confirm that no pages are missing or out of order), and that the documents reflect any last-minute changes you requested. A lot of paper gets passed around the table during execution—from your attorney to you to witnesses to a notary public back to your attorney and ultimately back to you—and it is possible for signature pages to get separated from their intended documents. Before you leave with signed documents in hand, do one final review to make sure that those documents are complete and in order.

Document Storage and Distribution

Once your documents are signed, what should you do with them?

1) Will

Your original Will should be stored with your other important documents. This can be in a safe deposit box (check to make sure the box won't be sealed at the time of your death; state laws vary), a fireproof safe in your home, or your filing cabinet. Some attorneys offer to hold originals at their offices; this may sound like a good option, but it raises some risks:

- The attorney's office may close or move without notice to you, leaving your survivors unable to locate your original Will. Let's say you live twenty or thirty years after your documents are executed. Will your attorney still be in practice?

- Your Will may be lost. A large law firm may have an organized, secure, dedicated storage area for original documents, but many smaller firms don't. Your original Will may be placed in your file, which may be moved to a "closed files" area of the file room after six months, then to a "permanent storage" area of the file room after five years, then to a third-party offside storage facility five years later. When you die ten years after that, what are the odds your file will be easily retrieved?

If your attorney offers to store your original documents, ask to see where they will be stored and how they will be tracked and protected. If you're not satisfied, keep them yourself.

Give a copy of your Will to your first named executor if you like, but in general no one else other than your attorney should need a copy.

2) Property power of attorney

Keep your original property power of attorney with your Will and let each named agent know where it's located. Since a photocopy (usually) has the same legal force as the original, you don't want numerous copies floating around unnecessarily.

3) Health care directive

Give a copy of the original to each named agent and your primary care physician. Many hospitals will accept a copy to hold on file; if there is a particular hospital you anticipate using, check to see if this is an option.

4) Trust

Give a copy to your trustee and, if they want one, to your accountant and your financial advisor.

Review Schedule

Your plan is a reality now, but don't forget that reality can change. You need to review your plan periodically to ensure that it still reflects your wishes and goals. How often should you review?

- If you have young children, review your plan annually. Think about how your children have changed over the past year and consider whether your choice for guardian is still the best choice, and consider whether the events of the year have raised concerns that warrant reconsideration of your distribution plan. Update the Information for Guardian form as appropriate.

- If you have adult children, review your plan at least every three years. Confirm that your distribution plan still makes sense in light of any changes (positive or negative) in each child's circumstances.

- If you have no children, review your plan at least every five years.

In addition to the above schedule, you should review your plan any time you experience one of the following life events:

- marriage
- divorce
- birth of a child or grandchild
- death of any beneficiary
- death of anyone named to a role
- significant change (positive or negative) in net worth
- retirement
- relocation to a different state or country

When you conduct your review, you are looking for decisions you made that no longer feel appropriate. The easiest way to accomplish a review is to step through the process you just completed and stop any time a decision you made originally gives you pause.

Communicating Your Plan

Technically, you're done—you have a well-considered plan reflected in legally sufficient and properly executed documents. There is one final step, though, that you should take before you pat yourself on the back: Communicate your plan to those who need or deserve to know.

By "communicate," I don't mean inform them that your plan is in place and leave it at that, and I don't mean leave a brief note to be read upon your death that will raise more questions than it answers. I mean sit down with them now and explain how your plan will work and why you made the decisions you made. In some cases, the discussion may be uncomfortable—particularly if it's with a beneficiary whose share will be limited or retained in trust—but they deserve to know and they deserve to hear it from you.

At the back of this guide are checklists to help guide your conversations. Completing these conversations will help ensure that your plan works effectively when the time comes.

Conclusion

I hope you will take a moment to consider what you have accomplished in the course of completing this guide. You now know who will act for you if you become disabled, and you know who will assist your loved ones after your death. You know who will receive your personal effects when you die and you know how your wealth will be used to benefit others long after you're gone. Most important, you know that you have given these decisions the thoughtful attention they deserve. You have done your best, and for that you should be congratulated.

It has been my honor to walk with you through your decision-making process, and I sincerely hope that this guide has been helpful.

APPENDICES

Appendix A: Estate Plan Blueprint

Roles

Executor

1) _____

2) _____

3) _____

Guardian

1) _____

2) _____

3) _____

The following should *not* be appointed guardian:

1) _____

2) _____

3) _____

Trustee

1) _____

2) _____

3) _____

Property Agent

1) _____

2) _____

3) _____

Health Care Agent

1) _____

2) _____

3) _____

Distribution of Property

1) Personal Property

_____ To my spouse (if applicable), otherwise as below

_____ Specific items to be included in my Will:

Item	Recipient
_____	_____
_____	_____
_____	_____
_____	_____

_____ I will leave a list

_____ Distribute everything else to these people:

_____

_____

_____

____ as they agree

____ as my executor decides

____ in this manner (take turns, auction, etc.):

_____

_____

_____

2) Specific monetary bequests

Recipient	$ amount
_____	_____
_____	_____
_____	_____
_____	_____
_____	_____

3) Residuary Estate

< Restate your plan from the Distribution section in whatever manner is easiest for you >

Provisions for Spouse

The portion of my residue allocated for my spouse should be

_____ Given to my spouse outright

_____ Held in trust for my spouse as follows:

Level of support:

_____ Minimal

_____ Maintain our current standard of living

_____ Whatever is in my spouse's best interests

Spouse's contribution:

____ I expect my spouse to work if possible.

____ I want my spouse to be able to stay home when our children are minors, but after that I expect my spouse to work.

____ I don't expect my spouse to work.

If my spouse remarries:

____ Consider the new spouse's financial resources.

____ Don't consider the new spouse's financial resources.

At my spouse's death, the remainder beneficiaries are:

Beneficiary	Dollar amt or %
____ Children	_____
____ Other individuals	
_____	_____
_____	_____
_____	_____
____ Charities	
_____	_____
_____	_____
_____	_____

Balance my spouse's interest against the remainder beneficiaries' interest as follows (make a mark at the appropriate point on the scale):

←——+——→

It's all about my spouse   *It's all about the remainders*

Provisions for Children

The portion of my residue allocated for my children should be split into shares:

_____ Immediately

_____ When my youngest child reaches age _____

_____ Never

_____ Other: _____

The shares should be

_____ equal

_____ unequal, as follows:

Child	Percentage
_____	_____
_____	_____
_____	_____

I do not intend to leave any of my residue to the following child/children:

_____

_____

_____

Child #1

The share for my child _____ should be:

_____ Given to this child outright

_____ Held in trust

Level of support:

_____ Minimal

_____ Moderate

_____ Liberal

_____ Other: _____

Is this child disabled? _____ Yes _____ No

Mandatory scheduled distributions:

Event (age, milestone, etc.)	Dollar amt or %
_____	_____
_____	_____
_____	_____
_____	_____
_____	_____

At the child's death, any remaining trust balance should be distributed to:

_____ The child's children, if any, _____ outright or _____ in trust

_____ The child's siblings

_____ Other individuals:

Person	Percentage
_____	_____
_____	_____
_____	_____

_____ Charities

_____

_____

_____

Specific concerns about this child:

_____

_____

_____

Additional comments about this child:

_____

_____

_____

_____

Child #2

The share for my child _____ should be:

_____ Given to this child outright

_____ Held in trust

Level of support:

_____ Minimal

_____ Moderate

_____ Liberal

_____ Other: _____

Is this child disabled? _____ Yes _____ No

Mandatory scheduled distributions:

Event (age, milestone, etc.)	Dollar amt or %
_____	_____
_____	_____
_____	_____
_____	_____
_____	_____

At the child's death, any remaining trust balance should be distributed to:

_____ The child's children, if any, _____ outright or _____ in trust

_____ The child's siblings

_____ Other individuals:

Person	Percentage
_____	_____
_____	_____
_____	_____

_____ Charities

_____

_____

_____

Specific concerns about this child:

_____

_____

_____

_____

Additional comments about this child:

_____

_____

_____

_____

Child #3

The share for my child _____ should be:

____ Given to this child outright

____ Held in trust

Level of support:

____ Minimal

_____ Moderate

_____ Liberal

_____ Other: _____

Is this child disabled? _____ Yes _____ No

Mandatory scheduled distributions:

Event (age, milestone, etc.)	Dollar amt or %
_____	_____
_____	_____
_____	_____
_____	_____
_____	_____

At the child's death, any remaining trust balance should be distributed to:

_____ The child's children, if any, _____ outright or _____ in trust

_____ The child's siblings

_____ Other individuals:

Person	Percentage
_____	_____
_____	_____
_____	_____

_____ Charities

_____

_____

_____

Specific concerns about this child:

_____

_____

_____

Additional comments about this child:

_____

_____

_____

<repeat for additional children as necessary>

Provisions for Other Beneficiaries

Beneficiary: _____

_____ Outright

_____ Hold in trust

Purpose: _____

_____

How funds should be used:

_____

_____

When trust terminates:

_____

_____

What to do with remaining funds at termination:

_____

_____

Beneficiary: _____

_____ Outright

_____ Hold in trust

Purpose: _____

_____

How funds should be used:

_____

_____

When trust terminates:

_____

_____

What to do with remaining funds at termination:

_____

_____

_____

Beneficiary: _____

_____ Outright

_____ Hold in trust

Purpose: _____

_____

How funds should be used:

_____

_____

When trust terminates:

_____

_____

What to do with remaining funds at termination:

_____

_____

Beneficiary: _____

____ Outright

____ Hold in trust

Purpose: _____

_____

How funds should be used:

_____

_____

_____

When trust terminates:

_____

_____

What to do with remaining funds at termination:

_____

_____

_____

Beneficiary: _____

_____ Outright

_____ Hold in trust

Purpose: _____

_____

How funds should be used:

_____

_____

_____

When trust terminates:

_____

_____

What to do with remaining funds at termination:

_____

_____

_____

<repeat for additional beneficiaries as necessary>

Appendix B: Communication Checklists

Executor:

____ Identity of attorney, accountant, financial advisor

____ Location of original Will and other financial documents

____ Burial/cremation/memorial service wishes

____ Basic outline of plan

____ Information about unusual assets

Guardian:

____ Discuss where children would live, housing options, etc.

____ Your goals for each child

____ Any challenges each child is presenting

____ Religious practices

____ Each child's talents, interests, and personality

____ Discipline philosophy

Trustee:

_____ Identity of attorney, accountant, financial advisor

_____ Assets

_____ Distribution plan

_____ Views on distribution standards, appropriate support, etc.

Beneficiary:

_____ Identity of executor/trustee

_____ Distribution provisions for that beneficiary

_____ Reasons for retention in trust, if applicable

_____ What you want your provisions for that beneficiary to accomplish

_____ Reasons for treating beneficiaries differently, if applicable

Health Care Agent:

_____ Views on heroic medical measures

_____ Views on experimental treatment

_____ Preferred living arrangements in the event of disability

Appendix C: Assets and Liabilities

as of _____, 20____

Real Estate

Address or Description: _____

Ownership: _____

Estimated value: _____

Estimated mortgage debt and lender, if applicable: _____

Address or Description: _____

Ownership: _____

Estimated value: _____

Estimated mortgage debt and lender, if applicable: _____

Address or Description: _____

Ownership: _____

Estimated value: _____

Estimated mortgage debt and lender, if applicable: _____

Life Insurance

Company: _____

Insured: _____

Amount: _____

Policy Owner: _____

Beneficiary: _____

Contingent beneficiary: _____

Company: _____

Insured: _____

Amount: _____

Policy Owner: _____

Beneficiary: _____

Contingent beneficiary: _____

Retirement Accounts/Plans

Type (IRA, 401(k), pension, etc.): _____

Participant: _____

Amount: _____

Beneficiary: _____

Contingent beneficiary: _____

Where Held: _____

Type (IRA, 401(k), pension, etc.): _____

Participant: _____

Amount: _____

Beneficiary: _____

Contingent beneficiary: _____

Where Held: _____

Type (IRA, 401(k), pension, etc.): _____

Participant: _____

Amount: _____

Beneficiary: _____

Contingent beneficiary: _____

Where Held: _____

Bank Accounts, CDs

Bank: _____

In whose name: _____

Amount: _____

Any beneficiary listed on account? If so, who? _____

Bank: _____

In whose name: _____

Amount: _____

Any beneficiary listed on account? If so, who? _____

Bank: _____

In whose name: _____

Amount: _____

Any beneficiary listed on account? If so, who? _____

Other investment accounts (brokerage accounts, mutual funds, etc.)

Where held: _____

In whose name: _____

Amount: _____

Any beneficiary listed on account? If so, who? _____

Where held: _____

In whose name: _____

Amount: _____

Any beneficiary listed on account? If so, who? _____

Where held: _____

In whose name: _____

Amount: _____

Any beneficiary listed on account? If so, who? _____

Where held: _____

In whose name: _____

Amount: _____

Any beneficiary listed on account? If so, who? _____

Other investment assets

Individual stocks (not in an investment account)

Company	# shares	Value

Individual bonds (not in an investment account)

Issuer	Value

Collections

Type	Value	Location
_____	_____	_____
_____	_____	_____
_____	_____	_____
_____	_____	_____
_____	_____	_____

Other significant assets (describe, including ownership interest and value):

Closely held business:

_____

_____

Beneficial interest in a trust:

_____

_____

Other:

_____

_____

Debts and liabilities

Description of debt: _____

Owed to: _____

Outstanding balance: _____

Secured by (if applicable): _____

Description of debt: _____

Owed to: _____

Outstanding balance: _____

Secured by (if applicable): _____

Description of debt: _____

Owed to: _____

Outstanding balance: _____

Secured by (if applicable): _____

Description of debt: _____

Owed to: _____

Outstanding balance: _____

Secured by (if applicable): _____

Appendix D: Information for Guardian

Use this form to tell your children's guardian things you would want him or her to know about your children if you were to die tomorrow. Fill out one form for each child and update it every year or so while the child is still a minor.

Child's name: _____

Child's current age: _____

Child's Physician: _____

Child's Dentist: _____

Closest relative (other than parents):

_____

Names of child's closest friends:

_____

_____

Favorite activities:

Current routine (bedtime, eating schedule, bath schedule, etc.):

Health status and concerns:

School experience (name of school and teacher, typical grades, most and least favorite subjects, behavioral concerns, special needs, etc.):

Extracurricular activities (lessons, sports, etc., including schedules):

Eating habits (favorite foods, food allergies, dietary restrictions, concerns about eating patterns, etc.):

_____

_____

Current disciplinary methods and how they work with this child:

_____

_____

Relationships with siblings:

_____

_____

Special talents and gifts:

_____

_____

Special challenges:

_____

_____

Appendix E: Information for Executor

Use this form to gather information that may be useful to your Executor.

Names of professional advisors:

Attorney:

Accountant:

Financial Advisor:

Social Security number:

Military ID, if applicable:

Location of important documents (e.g., safe deposit box at xxxxx Bank, desk drawer in home office, safe located in den, etc.):

Wishes regarding burial/cremation/funeral service:

Wishes regarding disposition of pets, if applicable:

Location of valuables in home:

Notify these people of my death (list people who might not otherwise be notified; include contact information):

Online accounts (e.g., Facebook, Twitter) to be deleted upon my death:

Account	UserID	Password
_____	_____	_____
_____	_____	_____
_____	_____	_____

Personal (non-financial) papers:

___ destroy upon my death

___ give to _____

Appendix F: Cheat Sheet

Beneficiary. A person or charity that will get something (benefit) from your estate.

Bequest. A gift.

Decedent. A dead person.

Estate Plan. At a minimum, an executed Will that determines what happens to your stuff when you die. Should also include powers of attorney and health care directives that will take effect during your lifetime if you become disabled.

Execution (of a document or plan). Signed with whatever formalities are required, e.g., witnesses or notarization.

Executor. The one who will settle your financial affairs when you die, including identifying and gathering assets, paying debts, and distributing the balance to those who are entitled to receive it.

Fiduciary. Someone entrusted to manage someone else's property. Executors, trustees, and property agents are all fiduciaries.

Living Will. An older form of a Health Care Directive (a/k/a health care power of attorney) which specifies what types of medical care you do and do not want to receive if you are terminally ill.

Living Trust. Same as a revocable trust.

Probate. A court process which is sometimes necessary after death to get the decedent's property where it needs to go.

Residue. Whatever's left. In the context of estate planning, it means the property that remains after debts and expenses have been paid and specific bequests have been satisfied.

Revocable trust. The most common type of trust used in estate planning. A revocable trust can be changed or revoked at any time until the person who created it dies.

Specific bequest. A gift from an estate or trust of a specific thing (such as a piece of jewelry) or a specific amount of money.

Trust. A trust is a legal entity established by an agreement between the person who is creating the trust (called a grantor, settlor, or sometimes trustor) and the person who will manage it (the trustee). Think of a trust as similar to a corporation—it's not an actual person, but it has rights and responsibilities under the law. In most cases, the trust "owns" property for the benefit of one or more real people and manages and distributes the property according to the terms of the trust agreement.

Trustee. The one who manages a trust.

Will. A document that lays out what should happen after you die, including who will settle your final affairs, who will raise your minor children (if you have any), and who gets your property. The validity of a Will is governed by state law, but it almost always has to be a written document and it almost always has to be signed and dated by the person creating it.

www.ingramcontent.com/pod-product-compliance
Lightning Source LLC
Chambersburg PA
CBHW081453170526
45166CB00008B/2414